On the Theory of
Achievement Test Items

John R. Bormuth *On the Theory*
of Achievement
Test Items

With an Appendix   *On the Linguistic*
by Peter Menzel   *Bases of the Theory*
of Writing Items

The University of Chicago Press   *Chicago*
and London

Standard Book Number: 226–06630–4
Library of Congress Catalog Card Number: 70–102071

The University of Chicago Press, Chicago 60637
The University of Chicago Press, Ltd., London

To my wife, Susie

Contents

Acknowledgments   ix

1   INTRODUCTION   1
Objective   1
Outline of the Book   3
Two Caveats   4
Summary   7

2   ADEQUACY OF CURRENT TEST
CONSTRUCTION METHODS   8
Two Methods of Constructing
Achievement Tests   8
Contrasts of the Two Procedures   10
Criterion Reference Tests   15
Formative Evaluation and
Programming Instruction   17
Summative Evaluation   20
Standardized Achievement Tests   23
Research in Instructional Theory   25
Instructional-content Analysis Theory   28
Summary   32

3   CONSTRUCTION OF
ACHIEVEMENT TEST ITEMS   34
Requirements of Item Transformations   34
Item Transformations   35
Linguistic Description Devices   36
Sentence-derived Items   39
Discourse-derived Items   50

4   ASSUMPTIONS AND METHODS IN
ITEM-WRITING RESEARCH   56
Selecting and Creating Items to be Defined   56
Assigning a Structure to the Instruction   57
Assigning a Structure to the Question   62
*Devising Rules to Relate
Items to the Instruction*   64

5   OBJECTIVES AND METHODS OF
RESEARCH ON ACHIEVEMENT TEST ITEMS   66
Item-writing Theory   66
Item-response Theory   68
Item-validity Theory   82
A Final Remark   83

APPENDIX: THE LINGUISTIC BASES OF THE
THEORY OF WRITING ITEMS FOR
INSTRUCTION STATED IN NATURAL LANGUAGE
Peter Menzel   87
Introductory Remarks   87
1. *Parts of Speech Analysis*   99
2. *Transformational Analysis*   115
3. *Sentence Types*   130
4. *Anaphora Analysis*   147
5. *Intersentence Syntax*   150

References   157

Index   161

Acknowledgments

When an author has finished his work and sits back to view it, he is likely to realize that, regardless of how creative and original it may appear to others, his contribution has been largely one of collecting and reorganizing the thoughts of others. He has discussed his ideas with others, and they have challenged them, augmented them, and encouraged their development. Others have bent the world around him, taking the children to the museum or relieving him of academic duties so that he could work. As a result, when the author finally sits down to acknowledge all this assistance, he must somehow thank large numbers of people who are all important to him, but he must do so in a limited space.

First, I wish to thank my family and colleagues, who tolerate my tendency to talk endlessly about my work. They actually listened, and their comments and challenges did much to shape the ideas I present here. Next I should like to thank Lee Cronbach for providing the Conference on Learning and Education, at which I first began to formulate the problem in its present form. Merlin C. Wittrock through the U.C.L.A. Research and Development Center provided occasions for thinking about these problems, but my debt to him is particularly great because of his long-term encouragement and his penetrating challenges of my ideas as I developed them.

Others have made clearly identifiable contributions. Robert Gagné asked me how my ideas related to his ideas. My answer is in chapter 5. Peter Menzel has done his best to keep me honest in the use of linguistic descriptors. David Wiley and Sue Meyer-Markle have given advice, counsel, and challenge more often than either suspects. And the works of Wells Hively and Richard Anderson have convinced me that this is not just a private hallucination. Benjamin Bloom, Frederick B. Davis, and Ralph Tyler, whose writings have taught me whatever I know about achievement measurement, pretty well round out the list of those to whom I owe gratitude. Except for one—Roberta—that intrepid secretary who with fingers of steel, the eye of an eagle, and the patience of an army sergeant got this manuscript into its final form.

Introduction 1

Education has come into the mainstream of our nation's activities, where it is being employed as a political instrument to solve social problems and as an economic instrument to supply industry and government with trained manpower. In both functions education has become vital to the attainment of national objectives, and consequently it has become a central area of concern in the making of public policy.

Inevitably, achievement testing has been drawn into playing a basic role in these activities. Congress and various private organizations are pouring huge sums of money into research aimed at the development of and the improvement of the designs for instructional programs. And they demand that the programs be tested both during and after development to determine their effectiveness and to justify the moneys spent. This research must make use of achievement tests, since they offer the only convenient method of observing the complex behaviors involved in instruction.

This has suddenly placed new demands upon the technology of achievement testing and has cast the achievement test specialist in a new role. Traditionally, the test specialist has, rather narrowly, regarded himself as a supplier of helpful procedures and hints to classroom teachers. His methods were specifically designed to transmit a few simple skills to teachers having little technical background and few resources for learning and applying sophisticated procedures. It mattered little if the testing procedures were easily affected by the biases and idiosyncrasies of the teacher. Subjectivity could be regarded as their virtue. The individual teacher was almost the sole consumer of the test results, and his biasing of those results only meant that they agreed with his conceptualizations of the behavior he was trying to shape in his students. Nor did it matter that commercially prepared

1

tests were suited only for comparing the relative achievements of children in rather gross terms. He was constantly observing the child's responses and could, if necessary, provide detailed accounts of the skills he had or had not acquired.

But the upsurge of public interest in education has suddenly confronted the achievement test specialist with a different set of problems. He is now being asked to construct achievement tests which can provide evidence sufficiently unbiased to be taken as evidence in making decisions of public policy involving huge sums of money. The policy makers are asking the test specialist to supply them with answers to questions such as *Of the different items of content presented in a given instructional program what percentage have the students learned?* and *Of the programs available in a given area, which results in the greatest number of items of content learned per unit cost expended?* Tests which can effectively answer such questions must satisfy assumptions far more stringent than any ever before considered by the test specialist.

The test specialist is also being asked to devise methods of producing test items which are sufficiently rigorous to serve as the basis for scientific investigations of instruction. He is not being asked to supply the scientist with a few test items which, in the test specialist's introspective judgment, seem to test some underlying behavioral capability. The scientist has little interest in studying the inner life of the test specialist. Rather, the test specialist is being asked to provide the scientist with *descriptions* of classes of items which will permit the scientist to produce them himself and then determine what behavioral capabilities, in fact, underly the responses to those items. When the scientist has established this, he can then proceed to study the factors which influence the effectiveness of instruction.

In short, the achievement test specialist is suddenly being confronted with impatient demands that he cease regarding himself solely as a concocter of homey recipes for classroom teachers and start subjecting his art to the disciplined analysis necessary to raise it to the status of a systematic and useful science. Education has become too vital to human welfare, and achievement testing too central to the improvement of education, to permit achievement test writing to rest on anything but the soundest basis scentific methods can achieve.

The motivation for this book was the conviction that the current procedures for constructing achievement tests are too primitive to permit achievement tests to satisfy modern demands in anything approaching the rigorous manner required. The problem arises from the fact that, in the final analysis, the concepts and procedures traditionally employed in the construction of achievement test items are defined wholly in the private subjective life of the test writer, which makes achievement testing little better than a dark art. At a time when most of the behavioral sciences have long since incorporated operationalism into their methods of theory building, achievement test theory—if it can be said to be a theory at all—has remained rooted in the introspective techniques of the early nineteenth century.

The purpose of this book is to present and demonstrate an operational approach to the construction of achievement test items. The fundamental premise of this approach is that an achievement test item cannot produce meaningful results unless it can be related to and derived from the instruction by a set of operations. The operations themselves describe a set of publicly observable manipulations by which a test item is derived from the instruction. To those with some scientific sophistication it will be clear that what is to be advocated is the very basic and almost self-evident idea that achievement test items, like any other measuring device, ought to be operationally defined. And it will be claimed that when they are so defined many of the most serious limitations and restrictions on achievement tests can be removed and that questions in instructional theory previously considered beyond the reach of scientific analysis will be amenable to investigation.

OUTLINE OF THE BOOK

The object of chapter 2 is to make a case for the operationalization of definitions of achievement test items. It begins by describing both the traditional and operational approaches to the writing of achievement items. Then it discusses four of the major contrasts between the items produced by the two approaches. Finally, the major uses of achievement tests are discussed with respect to these contrasts to evaluate the relative merits of the two approaches.

Chapter 3 presents the results of a substantial amount of research which developed operational definitions for a large number of the classes of items commonly used to test achievement resulting from verbal instruction. There were two purposes in presenting these definitions. The first was to provide extensive illustrations of operational definitions of items and the second was to give the reader a *feel* for how one goes about devising an operational definition for a class of items. Although the definitions presented draw heavily upon structural linguistics, semantics, and logic, an effort was made to keep the discussion within the ken of a reader with little more than some determination and a little rusty high school grammar at his command.

The systematic discussion of item-writing theory is postponed till chapter 4, which outlines the objectives and major components of this theory and discusses some of the research methods by which the theory is developed. While some preliminary explorations of problems in item-writing theory are commenced in this chapter, the primary purpose was merely to conceptualize the field.

But in defining a new branch of theory within a field, one seldom leaves the rest of the field unaffected. In chapter 5 it is pointed out that the existence of an item-writing theory now makes it possible to launch scientific investigations of the behaviors underlying responses to various classes of achievement test items. This branch of test theory is labeled *item-response theory*. The chapter describes some of the important questions to be investigated and suggests several models and methods which are useful in these investigations.

The appendix to this volume, which was written by Peter Menzel, serves as a supplement to chapter 3. It was considered an important addition both because it provides an excellent treatment of the linguistic theory underlying the item definitions presented in chapter 3 and because it provides fairly comprehensive inventories of the syntactic structures of English—information which is essential in much item-writing research.

TWO CAVEATS

From the outset of this discussion two points should be clear. First, no attempt is made to deal with the question of how evaluation activities can or should be carried out in practical school settings. From the preceding remarks it can probably be surmised that the position taken here is that this question has been shortsightedly allowed to dominate the attention of test specialists to the point where the really basic needs of education have been ignored and that this neglect has precipitated the present crisis conditions in education—wherein there is an acute need for sound data upon which to base decisions of educational policy and instructional theory, but no adequate technology for obtaining those data. Rather, the remarks in this book are addressed to the prior and more urgent question, How should achievement tests be designed so that they can produce scientifically valid results? Ultimately, answering this question will produce far more practical benefits than attending to the immediate demands of the schools.

Second, it should also be kept clearly in mind that the basis for all the assertions which follow is the philosophical position taken to support all scientific operationalism. It would seem trite to recite the tenets of this position, since they have long since been incorporated into the fabric of theory building by the general scientific community.

Even achievement test specialists have at least nominally accepted operationalism. Yet, as will be shown, the fundamental concepts upon which achievement testing is presently based must be regarded as being basically subjective; so a brief explanation will be attempted.

To develop a science of achievement testing, the procedures for deriving items from the instruction must be operationalized. One way to do this is to regard the test item as a property of the instruction and the item as being obtained by performing some manipulation on the instruction. Thus, an operational definition of a class of achievement test items is a series of directions which tell an item writer how to rearrange segments of the instruction to obtain the items of that type. At no point may these instructions require the test writer to call upon his introspection nor may they permit him to exercise any options at his own discretion.

This is not to claim that intuition and introspection play no part whatever in developing operational definitions. It is necessary to conceptualize the kinds of behaviors that seem worth testing, and these initial conceptualizations are, in large measure, based upon intuition. It is also necessary to invent some examples of items which test the behaviors so that one can see the form of the items to be defined. This process, too, seems to require the use of introspection and intuition. But what *is* being claimed is that the concept of a class of items has an indefinite meaning until explicit rules can be provided for deriving items of that class.

When an operational definition is not provided for a class of items, the concept's meaning is indefinite in the sense that there is no way to definitely refute the claim that an item is or is not a member of the class. An impartial observer could not observe every step in the derivation of the item and certify that the steps had been performed correctly or incorrectly, because, in the absence of operational definitions, many of those steps take place solely within the head of the test writer.

When items are not operationally defined, responses to those items do not provide trustworthy evidence for purposes of making decisions on either instructional theory or public policy. In experiments which contribute to instructional theory the experimenter must report the effects that manipulating some variable in the instruction has upon responses to some class or classes of achievement test items. Unless the original experimenter can verify that his items are indeed of the type he claims, and unless other experimenters can construct items which they can certify are of that same type, other experimenters cannot independently claim that they have refuted or verified the original results;

5

and so the original study is worthless. Similarly, when those who make public policies call in results on achievement tests as evidence, they must be assured that the scores measure what it is claimed that they measure. But since there is no way for an impartial observer to verify that the test contains the types of items claimed, there is no way to give this assurance. Thus, the decision maker must regard the scores on achievement tests as representing uncertain and possibly biased evidence.

The problem goes much deeper than this. At the present time we seem to be in the position of having to accept the assertion that a test measures whatever the test writers claim it measures without recourse to definitive independent evidence. In the final analysis a test item bears a certain label just because the test writer and his associates say that that is what it measures. The only external evidence that may verify these claims is correlations of the scores on one writer's test with the scores on tests made by other test writers who claim that their tests measure the same thing or something slightly different. But correlational analyses of this sort almost invariably reveal significant correlations between the tests along with variation attributable solely to the individual tests. Since this evidence can be used to support either claim, it really supports neither. Further, it leaves open the question of whether any of the tests used measure what their authors claim.

This uncertainty about what an achievement test measures is due to an improper conceptualization of the question. Instead of viewing the matter as a proper subject for research, test specialists have taken the position that, if in their introspective judgment an item measures a particular behavior, they may apply that label to the item. This position not only implies that there really is some identifiable mental process corresponding to this label but also that this label can be affixed to the item on no better evidence than the authoritative statements of a test writer and possibly of a panel of other test writers who concur in his judgment.

It seems much more rational to recast the question as a problem for scientific investigation. That is, it seems more appropriate to start with a tightly defined category of items and then to proceed, through experimental manipulation of the instruction and the testing conditions, to systematically build a theory of the processes underlying responses to that class of items. However, this type of experimentation is not possible unless classes of items can be operationally defined, because there is no way for the scientist to confirm or refute the results of such studies, and therefore no way to test the truth of the sentences in his theory.

SUMMARY

As education has come to serve as a major determinant of our social and economic well-being, it has received increasing attention as a subject of public policy. This has led to the channeling of rather massive financial support into research and development projects directed at improving instruction. One of the less pleasant results of these projects has been the revelation of the shortcomings of achievement tests made by traditional methods. Results from these tests cannot be taken as unbiased evidence upon which to base decisions of public policy, because it is impossible to verify that the tests measure what their makers claim. Nor can they be used as evidence in deciding issues in instructional theory, because there is no way to refute or confirm the results of a study in which items made by traditional methods were used. The reason for these problems is that items made in the traditional manner are derived through the private intuition of the item writer rather than through a set of operations open to public inspection. This last claim will be explored in some detail in the next chapter.

Adequacy of
Current Test
Construction Methods

2

Two points are made in this chapter. First, current methods of making achievement tests must be abandoned because they contain irreparable flaws which make it impossible to defend almost any use to which they are put. Second, items derived from operational definitions contain none of these flaws and can provide a scientifically sound base for achievement testing. The argument will begin with a brief description of each of the two methods of constructing achievement test items; next the methods will be contrasted; finally, these contrasts will be applied to several of the major uses of achievement tests to show the relative merits of tests made by the two methods.

Two Methods of Constructing Achievement Tests

The steps involved in constructing traditional achievement tests are now well established in practice and widely agreed upon by test specialists in the field. For example, test specialists such as Bloom (1956), Davis (1964), Thorndike and Hagan (1955), and Tyler (1950) give roughly identical descriptions of these traditional procedures.

The first step consists in making a content outline of the instruction. The object is to make this outline in such a manner that all the content in the instruction can be classified somewhere in the outline. The content outline of a geography program, for example, might contain entries such as *place names, soil types, terrain features,* and *economic activities.* This outline is then used to form a table in which the content categories and the entries under each serve as row labels. No rules are given to specify how this outline is constructed; this matter is left instead to the discretion of the test maker.

The second step consists in making a behavior outline of the instruction. The entries in this outline refer to the types of response behaviors through which the student is expected to demonstrate his knowledge of the content referred to by the row labels. The categories in the behavior outline are designed to represent the full range of complexity of cognitive processes which supposedly underlie the responses to the items eventually constructed. The labels of the response categories include phrases such as *locate on a map, define or describe, state relationships, organize, evaluate,* and the like. The resulting behavior categories are then used to label the columns of the table. Many writers have suggested taxonomies of the behaviors they think should constitute the column headings, but the exact behaviors to be placed in the column headings for any given test are left to the test writer's judgment of what is appropriate. However, he is reminded that tests provide an important influence in shaping what is taught, and he is often encouraged to frame many items from among the more complex behaviors while limiting the number of those which test the simpler behaviors.

In the third step, the test writer constructs items for each of the cells in the table for which he feels his program warrants items. No rules are given for deciding whether a particular program warrants an item in a given cell. Nor are any rules given for deciding exactly how the test item should be phrased. The authorities (for example, see Davis 1964, p. 262) regard the writing of items to correspond to cognitive behaviors as an art which depends almost entirely upon the introspective insight, perseverance, ingenuity, and literary artistry of the test writer.

The final step consists in having a panel of judges review the entire procedure and the resulting test. The function of this panel is to verify the judgments made by the test writer. It is generally recommended that this panel be composed of persons trained in test construction and in the relevant subject matter area.

Next, consider the item-writing method being proposed here—the derivation of items using operational definitions. The term *item,* as it is used to refer to the products of operational definitions, refers to the question, the correct response, and the distractors in multiple-choice items. An operational definition describes the manner in which a class of items is derived from instruction. It has two major components: a set of operations by which a syntactic structure is assigned to the instruction and a set of operations performed on that syntax which transforms the relevant segments of the instruction into test items. In other words, the instruction itself is transformed into the questions and the responses through the manipulations referred to by the operations which constitute the definition.

The procedure for deriving *subject-deletion* questions provides an example. Stated in only its grossest outline, the procedure consists of two sets of operations. The first set specifies the procedure for identifying the subjects of all the sentences in the instruction. While this amounts only to the assignment of a grammatical syntax to the instruction, it will become apparent in chapter 4 that higher levels of syntax must also be used to define many classes of items. The second set of operations requires the test writer to delete the sentence subjects and replace each with the appropriate "wh- pro" word such as *who, what,* or *where.* The correct response is, then, either the constituent deleted or a derivative of it obtained through further definitions. When applied, for example, to the sentence *The boy rode the horse,* this procedure derives just the question *Who rode the horse?* and no other question from that segment of instruction. Other definitions would be required to derive even a question as similar as *Who has ridden the horse?*

The items are produced in an automatic fashion. That is, once it has been decided to use the class of items produced by a given definition, all the items of that class which can be derived from the instruction are produced. Specifically, the item definitions contain neither provisions for selecting the classes of items to be derived nor provisions for selecting the items to be used from the items which are generated.

CONTRASTS OF THE TWO PROCEDURES

There are four major contrasts between operational and traditional methods of deriving achievement test items, and seemingly every criticism leveled at traditionally made achievement tests is traceable to their features which stand in contrast to those of tests containing operationally derived items. These contrasts will first be described and then their consequences evaluated.

First, when operational definitions are used to generate items, the test writer has no options in how he phrases each item. The phrasing is entirely determined by the definition. One of the principal constraints placed on operational definitions of items is that, just for the definitions to be regarded as *acceptable,* two different test writers using the same definition and instruction but working independently must be able to replicate each other's items in every detail. But to be regarded as *satisfactory* the definition must be sufficiently explicit to allow the item-writing process to be completely automated. The principal object, of course, is not just to attain automation of item writing, though that too is a worthy objective, but rather to completely explicate the item-writing process itself.

Conventional item-writing techniques, on the other hand, place so few constraints on the item writer that it seems improbable that two item writers could replicate each other's results. Indeed, one major element of the procedure is not even definable in an operational sense.

The process of makng the content outline is offered by the achievement tests specialists as a device for identifying all the content that should be tested, and thereby supposedly insuring that two test writers will produce the same sets of items. This procedure breaks down immediately. There are no known rules for constructing outlines, so whatever outlines the test writers make are undoubtedly a product of their individual concept structures. And the outlines probably show the idiosyncrasies of the individual item writers. Hence the very device which is supposed to have the effect of removing variability among test writers is, itself, affected by individual differences among test writers. However, it should be stated that, at least in principle, the outlining procedure can be rigorously defined even though achievement test specialists have shown no disposition to attack the problem or even to recognize its existence.

Making the behavior outline, however, is probably not a definable procedure when it is approached in the traditional way. The categories in these outlines refer to behaviors such as *evaluation, comprehension,* and the like. These labels refer to mental processes, not to observable events. So when the test writer selects such a label, he is using it to refer to something which occurs only in his private mental life. While it may be reasonable to expect a single test writer to show some consistency in his concepts of the behaviors referred to by these labels, it is highly questionable whether the same labels mean the same things to two different test writers. It is true that achievement test specialists often give a list of examples of questions which to them seem to test the process referred to by a label. But here we encounter the problem of how that class of items is defined. Since the test specialists have never given a statement of the attributes shared by all the items testing what they conceive of as a class of behavior, in the final analysis the test writer is forced back upon his private, and probably idiosyncratic, introspections to define the classes of behaviors he includes in his behavior outline. This undoubtedly affects the behaviors the test writer will list in his outline as being appropriate for testing. However, even if two test writers should happen to list the same behaviors, it is entirely likely that the labels mean something different to each. Hence, the behavior outline also permits variability in the items a test writer chooses to write.

The second major contrast between the two methods of writing items is in the verifiability of the claims made by the labels given the items. It should be emphasized that the issue being discussed here is not whether the test writer is motivated to be truthful in his labeling practices. Rather it is the question of whether the method used to define

11

the items would *permit* him to be truthful. The labels given items derived by operational definitions refer only to the operations used to derive the items. For example, the label given the subject-deletion items described above refers just to the grammatical constituent deleted to form the question. More particularly, it does not refer to the type of behavior assumedly tested by those items. Since the labels given items operationally derived refer only to publicly observable operations, it requires but a trivial exercise to determine if the item is of the type explicitly claimed.

Quite the opposite is true of items derived in a traditional manner. Such items are labeled using both the content and the behavior labels. Because the outlining procedure is ill-defined, it is difficult to verify that an item measures the content claimed by the label. For example, suppose the content outline contained the heading *place locations* in the outline of the content of a geography program. A test writer could place *Saint Louis* under that heading with equal justification regardless of whether the instruction stated that Saint Louis was near the confluence of the Mississippi and the Missouri Rivers, was in the middle of the continent, or was the center of political controversy. But items based on these three statements might not be given the same label by others, and their basis for not doing so would be equally justified. Consequently, the particular content labels given items derived by traditional methods are a matter of judgment and are therefore often misleading to a test user or even to another test writer.

The part of the item label which refers to the behavior tested presents even more acute problems. The same item may test different processes in different people. For one person the item $9 \times 12 = \underline{?}$ may require only a rote memory process, for another a computational process, and for still another a count process, depending upon their respective instruction in mathematics. Explicitly, one of the several variables determining what process a given item tests is the relationship between the item and the instruction given the persons tested with that item. But traditional item-writing procedures do not identify these relationships, much less specify how the relationships correspond to the various processes. As a result, the identity of the process tested by items made by traditional methods has no necessary relationship to the behavior named in the label, and, even if the label were correct, there would be no way to refute claims that it was incorrect.

This contrast reflects a still more fundamental difference between the operational and the traditional approaches to item writing. The question of what process an item tests never arises in the operational approach, because it is regarded as of no concern whatever to an item writer. Instead, this question is thought of as the proper concern of a different branch of achievement test theory, one which relies upon the experimental analysis of behavior to verify its claims. The item writer, on the other hand, is concerned only with the question how the items are derived from the instruction, given that a class of items is desirable. Traditional test-writing methods completely confound the two issues by depending upon the test writer's introspection to insure that the items test the process referred to by the behavior label. Since his introspective processes are not open to public inspection, there is no way to verify the truth of the item's label.

The third major contrast between the two approaches lies in the manner of deciding whether or not to write a particular item. In the operational approach this is not regarded as a part of the *item-writing* procedure but rather as a part of the *test-design* procedure. When an item definition is applied to the instruction it automatically produces every item of that type it is possible to produce from that instruction. The question of what items to select from among those produced and the question of what definitions to apply depend upon considerations which deal with the purpose of the test, the resources available, and so on—all of which are external to the item-writing procedure. Thus, if it is decided to randomly sample the items produced or to use only those which provide maximum discrimination power among students of a given level of ability, rules of this sort can be formulated and applied; but they are not regarded as a part of the item-definition rules and must therefore be rationalized separately.

But in the traditional approach to item writing the separate acts of test design and item writing are confounded in very complex and irregular ways. The traditional item writer seldom, if ever, sets out to write every possible item of a given type in making a test over a program. Rather, he avoids writing items he considers *trivial, too complex, too simple, too wordy,* or otherwise undesirable. Similarly, he will often simply decide that he has produced as many items as he needs. His decisions on these matters are seldom explicit and are almost never rationalized. Thus, as the test writer generates items by traditional methods, he is implicitly designing the test, but doing so in a manner that is not open to inspection and rational review.

The fourth major contrast between the two approaches to test writing is the most abstract; yet it has the most profound consequences for determining the power and limitations of the tests made by the two approaches. This contrast deals with the degree to which the item-writing procedure permits us to identify and specify the *logical relevance* of the item to the instruction—that is, to specify the segment

13

of the instruction from which the item was derived and to state the exact manner in which the structure of the test item is related to the structure of the relevant segment of the instruction.

The concept of an item's logical relevance must be sharply distinguished from the concept of the item's empirical relevance to the instruction. To establish an item's empirical relevance to instruction it is necessary only to show that subjects who were exposed to the instruction perform better on the item than subjects not exposed to the instruction. Thus, in establishing an item's empirical relevance one deals only with the superficial observations of responses. But in demonstrating an item's logical relevance to the instruction one deals with the prior theoretical question of whether there is any reason for expecting an empirical relevance to exist. Hence, discussions of the logical relevance of items are, in fact, discussions of the fundamental theory upon which all testing is based, whether that theory is stated explicitly or is left in the form of intuition and introspection on the part of the test writer.

When items are derived through the use of operational definitions, it is easy to provide exact statements of the logical relevance of test items to the instruction. The item definitions always specify the type of segment of instruction to which they apply, and the statements contained in the definition describe the exact relationship between the structure of the item and the structure of the segment of instruction. For example, the definition of the subject-deletion items described above clearly states that the segment relevant to any of the items it generates will be a sentence. This means that the sentence considered completely in isolation from the rest of the instruction serves as a sufficient basis for the derivation of the item. The statements in the definition also describe the structure of the item (in this case, its grammatical structure), the structure of the relevant segment of instruction, and the procedure for transforming the one structure into the structure of the other. In more concrete terms, the statements in the definition describe the sentence as containing a subject and a predicate, the item as containing a wh- pro word and a predicate, and then it describes how the structure of the sentence is manipulated to produce the item. Hence, the logical relevance of any sentence-deletion item to the instruction is completely specified by the definition.

When traditional item-writing procedures are used, however, descriptions of item relevance are much less exact, being stated in terms of the subjective judgmental procedures used by the test writer and his review panel. The test writer, of course, probably does his best to assure that his items do pertain to the instruction, the judges probably exert every effort to achieve the same goal, and the items finally made probably are relevant to the instruction. But this relevance is established primarily through introspection exercised by the test writer and his panel of judges rather than through the use of operational procedures open to public inspection and capable of independent verification and replication.

CRITERION REFERENCE TESTS

Achievement tests made by traditional methods have been used to measure the growth in a student's attainment and to compare his level of attainment with the levels reached by other students and norm groups, but they have generally been regarded as useless for determining the effectiveness of instructional programs. Glaser (1963), however, pointed out that it is not very useful to know how one student compares with others or whether his present performance exceeds his earlier performance, for few important policy and instructional decisions can be based upon such information. What is urgently needed is some way to compare the student's score with the criterion of mastery of the content. Information of this sort provides a means of determining in an absolute sense how well the student is performing and whether or not he needs additional instruction. It also provides a means of determining how effectively the instructional program teaches the content specified in the objectives. Glaser called such tests *criterion reference tests* to distnguish them from the *norm reference tests* currently in use.

It would be utterly indefensible to attempt to make such tests using traditional item-writing techniques, for a criterion reference test must meet criteria the traditionally made tests are unable to meet. To begin with the simplest case, interpreting a test score as being solely a function of the properties of the instruction requires that we assume that a test item has some fixed relationship to the instructional program. This simply is not so with items made by traditional methods, wherein it is perfectly permissible for the test writer to alter the phrasing, the vocabulary, and the alternative answers in any way he chooses. It is a commonly observed phenomenon in test writing that altering the form of an item has some effect on its difficulty. Since these alterations are left entirely to the discretion of the item writer, the difficulty of the items and, therefore, the magnitude of the scores on the tests are, in part, a function of the biases and linguistic idiosyncrasies of the person writing the test. Hence, scores on tests using items made by traditional methods measure not just the properties of the instructional program but also the properties of the person who happened to write the items.

It hardly needs pointing out that tests composed of items derived

15

through the use of operational definitions can easily meet this criterion. The item form is entirely fixed by the instruction and the definitions employed. The test writer's options are eliminated, and thus any variances attributable to his behavioral disposition are also eliminated.

Criterion reference tests also involve the assumption that the items in the test either exhaust or form a representative sample of the set of all possible items that can be derived from the instructional program being evaluated. Obviously, a score on a criterion reference test would be uniterpretable if the items were drawn in such a fashion that they could be biased to contain the easiest or the most difficult items which could be derived from the instruction. This can easily happen with tests made by traditional methods, since the test writer is given wide latitude in choosing the items to be written. Furthermore, it is commonly observed that test writers deliberately bias their tests, ignoring large numbers of the items that could be derived on grounds that those items are trivial, wordy, too simple, too complex, and so on.

Also, items made by traditional methods cannot be used to evaluate the difficulty of a program. The test maker cannot make a test containing all possible items from the program, because he has no rules in traditional test-making methods to tell him how many there are. Thus, he must draw a sample of the items for his tests. But if he should do so, he could not claim that his sample was an unbiased representation of all the items he could have made. Indeed, common observations of the habits of test writers suggest that his sample would probably be biased.

This is not to claim that an instructional program cannot be evaluated by using, say, just one or two classes of items rather than every conceivable type of item. Quite the contrary, it seems highly likely that many classes of items may turn out to be of little interest in measuring achievement. Rather, it is to be claimed that, for those classes of items which *are* selected for testing, the items included in the test must be an unbiased sample.

It should be emphasized that the faults which cause items made by traditional means to fail to satisfy this assumption are irremedial. Since the traditional test-writing methods provide no means of determining when all possible items have been produced, there is no way to determine whether the sample included in the test is biased or not. Any attempt to remedy this defect by constructing such rules would fail. There is no way to operationally define the behavior labels which name the classes of items, because these labels refer to the subjective inner states the test writer thinks he perceives when he engages in introspection about the kinds of processes an item requires him to use. Therefore, it is impossible to define populations of items when traditional methods are used.

Items generated from operational definitions easily meet this criterion. The application of a definition to the instruction automatically produces a population of items. Structures are assigned to the instruction, and the item definitions apply only to specified structures. This also makes it easy to verify that the population is exhausted and that an item is a legitimate member of that class. This amounts to no more than checking for clerical errors. Hence, since the members of an item population are enumerable and nonarbitrary, drawing a random sample from the population of all possible items in that class has a definite operational meaning.

In summary, important kinds of instructional decisions must be based on the kind of information obtained from criterion reference tests, but it is impossible to make such tests from items produced by traditional methods. The items in a criterion reference test cannot reflect the idiosyncrasies of the test writer, but rather they must reflect only the properties of the instruction from which they were derived. Also, the items actually used in a test must either exhaust the population of items which constitutes the set of all possible items that can be derived from the instruction or they must be a representative sample of that population. Items made by traditional methods fail to meet both criteria. On the other hand, items derived using operational definitions satisfy both criteria.

FORMATIVE EVALUATION AND PROGRAMMING INSTRUCTION

Achievement tests are widely used to test the effectiveness of instructional programs as the programs are being developed. The practice of instructional programming makes what is perhaps the most extensive use of achievement tests for this purpose. In this activity the instructional programmer constructs items which he hopes will systematically test all the content being programmed and then puts the program through a series of teaching-testing-revision cycles until the students demonstrate a criterion level of performance on the criterion tests. Cronbach (1963) and Scriven (1967) have called this type of procedure *formative evaluation*.

It should be obvious from the preceding discussion of criterion reference tests that the use of tests made by traditional methods is indefensible in formative evaluation. In formative evaluation the object is to be able to interpret the test score as representing a property of the instruction. But because of the numerous options left to the discretion of the item writer when traditional test-writing methods are used, and because traditional methods provide no way to define populations of items and to enumerate the members of those populations, scores on traditionally made tests must be interpreted as measuring, in some unknown proportion, the properties of the test writer. Hence, this use of traditionally made tests is illegitimate.

But the use of traditionally made tests is barred for still another reason. The traditional test-making procedures do not provide an effective method for determining the logical relevance of the items to the instruction. The instructional programmer initially makes and administers his tests for the purpose of determining the effectiveness of specific segments of his program. It is his intention to revise those portions of the program which produce poor results. Thus, he must be able to identify the segment of instruction to which each of his items is relevant.

But since he has had to use traditional test-making methods, he is forced into the position of being unable to identify with certainty the portion of the program relevant to a given item. The items are derived from the matrix of behaviors and content by an unspecified procedure, and the relationship between the matrix and the instruction has an unspecified character. This leaves the relationship of the item to the instruction too vague and undefined to enable him to make anything but the weakest claims that he can identify the segment of instruction to which a given item is relevant. Hence, he is unable to justify the use of the items appearing in his tests, and he is unable to justify altering a particular segment of text on the strength of the error rate found on one of those questions.

Programmers have recognized this problem, and they have attempted to solve it by ignoring the instruction altogether in deriving their items. Instead the programmer begins by listing statements of the objectives he is trying to achieve with his program, stating these objectives behaviorally as test items. Presumably, his reasoning is that, since there is an uncertain relationship between the objectives and the instruction and another uncertain relationship between the instruction and the items, he can remove one degree of freedom from the uncertainty by deriving his items directly from the objectives. He then sets out to shape the instruction in such a way that student performance on his test is maximized.

Actually, this procedure is not a real solution. Scriven (1967) has already pointed out the source of one of the major difficulties. The behaviorally stated objectives, which are actually test items, may not fully represent the abstract objectives the program designers had in mind, for the rules for deriving test items from abstract objectives are no better specified in traditional test theory than the rules for deriving test items from the instruction. Hence, the practice of beginning with behaviorally stated objectives simply replaces the question of whether the test items are logically relevant to the instruction with what may be an even more difficult question of whether the test items are logically relevant to the abstract objectives of the instruction.

The use of behaviorally stated objectives introduces another serious problem. The object of evaluation is not merely to find out something as narrowly limited as how well the instruction accomplishes the program designer's objectives. Evaluation projects should also find out what the program actually teaches. In view of the fact that there are no precise rules which permit program writers to derive instruction perfectly representing the abstract objectives set out for the program, it is not only possible to obtain programs which fail to achieve the objectives desired, but worse, it is possible to obtain programs achieving objectives which would be considered highly undesirable by them, the writers, and potential users of the program. The well-known case of the modern physics program which resulted in vastly improved achievement in the students taking the course but also in drastically reduced numbers of students taking the course is a case in point. When program writers base their evaluation only upon behaviorally stated objectives, they necessarily place themselves in the position of having to ignore the possible side effects of instruction.

This problem now appears much more serious than was formerly realized. Holland (1967) demonstrated that instructional programs contain large amounts of instruction which are irrelevant to the test items regarded by programmers as behavioral statements of the objectives of their programs. He carefully examined twelve different instructional programs and deleted those segments of the instruction which subjectively seemed irrelevant to the test questions in those programs. Then he gave subjects both the deleted and the undeleted versions of the programs. He found that he was able to delete from 10 to 75 percent of the words in various of the programs without detectably increasing the error rates on the items. An obvious interpretation of these results is that the programs included much content which was irrelevant to their behavioral objectives.

A much more defensible practice would be to derive the items directly from the instruction. This would assure that what the program in fact contained would be evaluated. Furthermore, the fact that the test derived in this manner failed to contain items the program designers thought of as representing their objectives or that the test contained items they thought of as testing skills they did not want to teach might be sufficient reason for changing the instruction.

The use of operationally defined items presents none of these problems. As was shown in the discussion of criterion reference tests, scores on tests made from operationally defined items may be interpreted as reflecting just the properties of the instruction permitting the evaluator to avoid the influences test writers are ordinarily permitted to exert on the scores of traditionally made tests. The fact that the logical relevances of operationally derived items are explicitly stated in the definitions permits the program writers to state precisely what segment of the instruction produced the responses on an item, and to justify the revisions they make to the programs. And finally, the fact that operational definitions derive items from the instruction itself assures that the tests will provide data for evaluating what was actually taught.

SUMMATIVE EVALUATION

Another function achievement tests should serve is in the evaluation of intact programs. After a program has been constructed, it is desirable to supply the potential consumer and the agency financing the program's development with descriptions on how well the program as a whole performs. This is called *summative evaluation*. Summative evaluation studies may (*a*) seek only to report how efficient one program's instruction is or (*b*) compare the efficiency of one program with the efficiencies of major competing programs. These two types of evaluation are referred to, respectively, as *time-trial* and *horse race* studies. Cronbach (1963) and Scriven (1967) have discussed many of the problems encountered in these studies. What will be discussed here is the relative merits of using tests obtained by traditional and by operational methods.

Insurmountable problems are encountered when traditionally made tests are employed in a time-trial evaluation study. The objectives of time-trial studies are to identify the content taught by a program and then to measure and report either the time required for students to reach a given criterion level of performance or the level of mastery reached in a fixed period of time. As a result of the preceding discussions, many of the problems encountered in a time-trial study should be apparent. A time-trial evaluation requires the use of a criterion reference test, and it has already been demonstrated that criterion reference tests cannot be made using traditional test-writing techniques.

The time-trial study directly involves an interesting and important problem which has been discussed only indirectly up to this point. That is, to carry out a time-trial study, it is necessary to have some means of identifying the *items of content* taught in a program so that they can be counted. The object of time-trial studies is to measure the efficiencies of programs, and measures of efficiency always express the ratio between the number of units produced and some measure of the cost of producing those units. In the case of instruction this would have to be the ratio between the number of units of content learned and the time or dollars expended on securing their learning. Obtaining such a ratio is a basic essential of a time-trial study, since it would be meaningless to report that students reached a criterion of, say, 90 per cent of mastery during 300 hours of instruction unless we had some idea of the magnitude of the learning task on which they had displayed this performance.

This is an important problem partly because the advancement of the design of instruction from its current status as a subjective art to the status of an engineering science depends upon the solution of this problem. The basis of an engineering science is the capability of evaluating the relative merits of alternative designs. This evaluation cannot be done by considering only the benefits received from selecting a given design alternative or only the costs which accompany those benefits. Rather the two measures must be expressed as a ratio. But so far we have been unable to assess the merits of alternatives in the design of instruction because we have been unable to count items of content. We are therefore unable to assess the relative costs of alternatives by expressing their consequences in terms of items of content learned per dollar expenditure. What makes this an interesting problem is that apparently the operational approach to item writing provides a method of defining and counting items of content.

An item of content can be given a clear operational meaning. The definition of an item of content is based upon the proposition that an item of content exists only if it can be tested. Hence, the number of items of content existing in a segment of instruction corresponds to the number of *different* test items which can be derived from that segment. A further distinction should be made between items of instructional content and items of instrumental content. Consider the sentence *Joe rode the horse* and the questions *Who rode the horse?* and *By whom was the horse ridden?* It can be shown by using the arguments presented in chapter 3 that both questions test the same structure in the sentence. An instructional structure which is potentially testable with one or more items is defined as an item of instructional content. But an accounting of content must also recognize the fact that, in addition to learning the instructional content, the student must learn whatever skills are required uniquely by questions in order to answer the types of questions used to test the instructional content. An element of *instrumental content* is represented by each different type of test item actually used to test the instructional content in the segment of instruction.

It is fairly easy to count the number of instructional and instrumental items of content in a program when operational item definitions are used. The item definitions contain the rules necessary to identify the structures underlying the instruction, and the rules also specify the structures from which items may and may not be derived. Hence, items derived from operational definitions can be used for time-trial evaluation studies.

However, it seems unlikely that traditional item-writing methods could be used for the same purpose. The number of items written for an instructional program seems to depend upon the number of entries in the content matrix made for the program. But since the number of entries and even the number of columns and rows of the matrix are left to the judgments and introspections of the test writer, it is difficult to see how a reliable counting procedure could be developed for use with traditional techniques of item writing.

In horse race evaluation studies the object is to contrast two instructional programs. Here the achievement test writer encounters all the problems characteristic of time-trial studies plus a few more. Since this fact alone indicates that tests made by traditional methods cannot be used for these purposes, this part of the discussion serves more to further test the power of tests made by operational methods than to evaluate traditional methods of test construction.

The first problem presented by a horse race evaluation study is the fact that two programs nearly always differ in content. Hence, when the test writer prepares items appropriate for just one of the programs he will nearly always obtain items testing content not taught in the other programs and omit items testing content actually taught by the other programs. Thus, he is faced with the problem of assuring that the items he uses are impartially representative of all the programs being evaluated.

With conventionally made tests, this is an impossible task. Since there is no operational way to verify that an item is or is not relevant to the instructional program, the test writer can only appeal to the potential consumers of the programs to have faith in his honesty and skill for assurance that the tests are not biased to favor one program. When operational methods are used, however, it becomes a simple matter to determine the programs to which an item is relevant. When the identical item can be derived from two programs, it is relevant in some way to both programs. The items can then be labeled and grouped to show the programs to which they pertain. This not only makes it possible to compare the programs with respect to the content common to both programs but also to contrast them with respect to their unique content. When an estimate of the programs' content-to-cost ratio is also given, a potential consumer has much of the data required to make fairly sound judgments about the relative merits of the programs.

A second problem arises from the fact that any one item may test quite different things depending on the instruction. Thus, asking for the spelling of a given word may require a student who was previously drilled on the word merely to recite from rote memory a string of letters but require a student who was not taught the word to analyze it into syllables and phonemes and then to apply his phonics knowledge to the task. Such items are not easily identified using traditional test-writing methods. They are, however, easily identified when operational definitions are used. To derive the item from one instructional program, one item definition would have to be used, but deriving it from the other program would require the use of a different definition.

The use of operationally defined items in conducting horse race and time-trial evaluation studies was examined not so much to contrast those items with traditionally made items as to demonstrate the important new tasks operationally defined items are able to perform. It was of only secondary importance to contrast the two item-writing methods at this point because it has already been shown that criterion reference tests cannot be made from conventionally written items, and both kinds of evaluation studies require the use of criterion reference tests. One of the new measurement capabilities is the possibility of expressing the efficiency of an instructional program in terms of cost per item of content acquired by the students.

STANDARDIZED ACHIEVEMENT TESTS

To yield interpretable results, standardized achievement tests too must make use of operationally defined items. It is true that the scores on criterion reference tests are used to evaluate instruction, whereas the scores on standardized achievement tests are used to evaluate students, but the use of the score is not relevant to this question. The relevant fact is that the object of both kinds of tests is to measure what the student has gained from his instruction.

The items in standardized achievement tests must be relevant to the student's instruction. There is no way to interpret a test score if an unknown proportion of the items test content not included in that student's instruction. The score cannot be compared with the scores of students in the test's norm group, because many of the students in the norm group would have been subjected to many different instructional programs. Part of the variability in their scores, then, would be due to the fact that greater or lesser proportions of the items test content contained in their instruction. Thus, unless it can be demonstrated that the items in the test were relevant to the instruction of both the student being evaluated and the students in the norm group, the score must be regarded as confounded.

It is not sufficient merely to show that relationships exist between the items in a test and the instruction of the students. It is also necessary to demonstrate that the form of the relationship between a given item and one of the instructional programs is identical to the relationships between that item and each of the other programs. It was pointed out earlier that it is possible for what appears to be the same item to test two quite different kinds of content. For example, asking one student to pronounce a word may require only the recall of an association learned in a paired-associate task whereas presenting the same word to a student who has not been given look-say instruction on that word might test the phonics content of his instruction.

It is probably true that there are a number of factors other than the relationship between an item and the instruction which influence the nature of the process underlying a student's response to an item. It is probably also true that the same student may at one time employ one process and the next time he is presented with the identical item employ a different process. The factors responsible for these behavior alternations are as yet poorly understood. But a fundamental precondition for arguing that an item tests the same content for two different students is that it can be shown that the item has the same relationship to the instructional histories of both. If it is not possible for the test specialist to show at least logical similarities in the way the two students *could* arrive at the answer to the question, he has no grounds whatever for asserting that the item does, in fact, test the same content for both students. In the absence of complete instructional histories it must at least be shown that the item has the same relationship to the instructional programs to which they have both been subjected.

At this point it hardly seems necessary to point out that the available standardized tests use items generated by traditional methods and that these items cannot be shown to be relevant to instruction, much less to bear a relationship of a particular form. It should also be obvious that operationally defined items can perform both functions and are therefore the kind of items most suitable for use in standardized achievement tests.

RESEARCH IN INSTRUCTIONAL THEORY

Research in instructional theory has been greatly limited by the fact that items made by traditional methods do not produce data which are adequate for deciding theoretical issues. The purpose of instructional theory is to describe how variables of instructional programs influence a student's achievement of the content of that instruction, and hence to provide the scientific basis for a technology which is capable of designing more efficient instructional programs. Experiments in instructional theory have commonly manipulated instructional variables such as the associative-strength or conceptual relationships among the words in the instruction and then observed the influences these manipulations produce upon some measure of learning.

The researcher's inability to utilize achievement test items has prevented him from studying the effects instructional variables have on the complex cognitive behaviors which constitute the most important outcomes of instruction. To date, the only scientifically defensible experiments in instructional theory have used simple learning tasks such as paired-associate learning, concept identification, and association tasks as their dependent variables, none of which provides anything more than information about some of the simple components of the complex cognitive behaviors which seem to underlie responses to ordinary achievement test items.

There are two principal reasons why items made by traditional methods do not provide scientifically valid evidence upon which to base decisions in instructional theory. The first is that the results of experiments cannot be verified. The basic maxim of theory building is that a statement is meaningless unless it is possible to imagine an experiment in which that statement can be refuted if it is false. When a researcher makes a generalized statement based on the results of an experiment, he is proposing to add that statement to the theory. This statement is of the form *An increase in instructional variable A causes an increase (or decrease) in correct responses to items of type B.*

When the items are made by traditional methods, this statement cannot be verified because a second investigator could not be certain that he could make the same type of item. The first experimenter wrote items which, in his introspective judgment, tested the mental process named in the label *B* of the items. The second investigator must construct that type of item in the same way, using his own introspective judgments, thereby finding himself in the position of having to certify that his mental events match those of the first experimenter. Since there is no way to certify this, there is no way for him to construct the same type of items as the first experimenter, and, therefore, no way for him to subject the first experimenter's statement to an experimental verification. Hence, statements based on data obtained from items made by tradtional methods cannot be used to decide issues in instructional theory.

Test specialists have attempted to avoid this problem in the past by having a panel of judges inspect and discard those items on which they could not agree about the proper classification. This merely enlarges the problem by changing the question Are the introspections of two individuals identical? to the question Are the introspections of two panels identical? But it leaves unchanged the basic fact that there is no publicly observable way to systematically check each of the operations by which the items are derived and verify that the operations were performed in the same way by independent investigators.

The second reason why items made by traditional methods do not provide valid evidence in experiments is that they do not provide the experimenter with either a theory for claiming that his responses were caused by his instructional stimuli or a way to specify the range of cognitive behaviors he is observing. It is inconceivable that an experimenter would use for his dependent variable test items which could not rationally be related to his instructional stimulus. Any result he obtained would have to be regarded as fortuitous. Nor is it likely that he would not wish to specify as narrowly as possible the type of cognitive behavior he is observing. Leaving the response unspecified would make his study meaningless. Operationally defined items facilitate the experimenter's work in both respects.

Given a single item which is in some way relevant to a segment of instruction, it is possible to develop an explicit theory which describes the nature of that relevance. In effect, the theory describes how the item is derived from the instruction, how the response is derived from the instruction, and how the question elicits the response. This description provides the necessary logical or theoretical basis for believing that the instruction *could possibly* lead to the correct response. When no reasonably believable theory of this sort can be constructed, the experimenter is not justified in using the item in his experiment. For example, should we observe that every time the bus driver applies the brakes to the bus we are riding in a cloud passes between us and the sun, the more rational among us are apt to reject a theory which claims that the application of the brakes caused the sun to be obscured, and we would defend our position with the assertion that there is no reasonably believable theory which asserts that cloud movements respond to the pressing of a brake pedal. Test items and their responses must exhibit this same logical relevance.

The claim that a response to an item arises from a particular underlying cognitive process is given initial credence in a similar fashion. The investigator makes explicit his concept of the operations involved in the cognitive process, expressing them in some symbolic form. Next, he develops a procedure for deriving from the insruction the answer to the question, expressing this procedure, also, in symbolic form. Then he shows that identical statements appear in both his description of the process and his description of the response derivation procedure. If neither description contains statements describing impossible events, his claim must be granted initial credibility.

The argument establishing credibility for the claim that a single process underlies the responses to all the items in a set is established in much the same way. First, the derivations of each item's responses are given in explicit statements. Then it is shown that the descriptions for all items share identical statements.

It is generally accepted that items of the same type (that is, items derived in the same way) permit a student to answer them using just a restricted number of different cognitive behaviors. This belief is supported by more or less systematic observation. At the most subjective level, traditional test makers find a fair-to-good amount of agreement among their judges when they ask the judges to sort items into categories according to the cognitive processes required to answer the items. Experience in developing operational definitions for items provides explicit confirmations of this observation: items which appear subjectively to test the same processes often have identical or similar derivations; items which seem to test different processes exhibit marked contrasts in the way they are derived; and it usually taxes the resources of the investigator to provide descriptions of more than two or three alternative methods for deriving the answer to an item. Hively et al. (1968) provided still more rigorous confirmation of this observation. When he administered several classes of operationally defined items to subjects, he found that there was relatively less variability among the difficulties of the items derived in the same way than between items having differing derivations. Hence, there are grounds for the general belief that when the investigator specifies the type of item he is using he is also specifying to some degree the type of cognitive behavior he is observing.

The advantages the operationally defined item gives the experimenter in these respects are impressive. The definition provides him with a ready-made theory of how the item and the response relate to the in-sruction. His claim that his items all test the same underlying process is easily given initial credibility. Because they were all derived through the use of the same operational definition, their derivations all contain identical statements. And, since the definitions are always explicit, his theories are also explicit. Finally, the item definitions provide him with rigorously replicable categories of items by which he can specify the range of responses observed.

The same is not true of items derived by traditional methods. Since the items are generated by subjective methods it is difficult to estab-lish credibility for the claim that the items are relevant and homogenous. Should the experimenter for some reason choose to derive his items by traditional methods and then set out to establish their credibility, he would observe the interesting result that he had developed operational definitions for his items.

This topic should not be left before one recognizes that the responses to any item under various circumstances probably represent decidedly different cognitive behaviors. In the area of achievement testing these circumstances are as yet poorly understood. However, as in the other branches of experimental psychology, it seems possible for the in-structional theorist to design experiments and use multistage testing designs to permit him to observe exactly the cognitive behaviors he wishes to examine when he uses achievement test items.

These facts have long been understood in most branches of experi-mental psychology. In paired-associate learning, for example, the test list is often simply the stimulus list. Since this practice represents the simplest possible relationship between the item and the instruction, there is little difficulty in building a logical theory for expecting the instruction to produce a response to the test items. In studies of transfer the relationship between the training stimulus and the test stimulus is also made perfectly explicit. That is, the test stimulus is some specified transformation of the training stimulus. When the operational approach to achievement test items is followed, achievement test items simply represent still more complex types of transfer tasks requiring somewhat more complex transformations for deriving the test tasks from the instructional stimuli. When the traditional item-writing approach is used, these relationships are obscured and no logical basis for valid experiments can be found.

INSTRUCTIONAL-CONTENT ANALYSIS THEORY

Traditional test-writing practices have probably had their most dele-terious effects in content analysis theory, where they have not only imposed an inappropriate and unproductive framework upon the field but also effectively prevented the development of a useful body of empirical research. Instructional-content analysis theory attempts to identify the items of content in an area of instruction, to operationalize those items of content by developing testlike tasks which provide practice in the skills corresponding to each item of content, and then to identify the hierarchical and other types of transfer relationships existing among the items of content. The object of the theory is to provide the scientific basis for selecting and sequencing the content of instruction.

Traditional test-writing practices have imposed upon content analysis an inappropriate framework. To see how this has happened it is first necessary to understand that the resources of achievement test theory impose an absolute limit on the content analyst's ability to deal with the phenomena he studies. Ideally, the analyst begins by examining the structure of the content in a subject matter area in order to identify each of the individual behaviors a student must learn if he is to master the content. It is, supposedly, only then that the analyst devises test items corresponding to each item of content, items which presumably force the student to employ the behavior corresponding to the item of content. It would obviously be incorrect to reverse this order of operation, since adopting a theory of testing first would necessarily impose the theory of testing upon the analysis of the content.

In actual practice, however, the analyst is limited by the test-writing methods made available to him by achievement test specialists. The analyst cannot identify an item of content unless he has some hope of devising a test item which forces the behavior corresponding to the item of content. The item of content plus the test item provides him with his only means of referring to the behavior he has conceptualized. The responses to the item provide him with his principal source of empirical evidence for constructing theories about the hierarchical and other transfer relationships among the behaviors he is studying. And finally, in the absence of test tasks corresponding to each of the items of content, the analyst can provide no means of giving students practice in the behaviors corresponding to the content and no means of obtaining the information necessary to design instruction and adapt it to the needs of individual students. So, regardless of the order in which the content analyst ought to proceed, he must proceed by first finding out what kinds of items he can write and how he must go about writing them. He cannot possibly proceed in any direction not permitted by the achievement test item-writing procedures made available to him by the test specialist.

Current test-writing procedures force the analyst to impose on his content the psychological theories of the test specialists. The test specialists have worked out elaborate taxonomies identifying what they suppose are the cognitive processes involved in instruction in all areas of content. And to employ their test-writing techniques it is necessary to adopt some such schematization of cognitive processes because, in this procedure, an item is defined not just by the content it tests but also by the kind of cognitive process it presumably tests. In other words, the test specialist has traditionally assumed that the cognitive process is determined by the test writer, not that it is implicit in the form and content of the instruction. He argues that it is the tests that determine what the students will learn. The objectives of the instruction designers and the structure of the instruction count for nothing in this view. Consequently, it is the item writer himself who determines what cognitive processes the students must employ to master the content of a given area of instruction.

This has left the content analyst with almost no job to do. There is no point in the analyst's attempting to determine what cognitive processes are required for mastery of the content. The processes are not designed into the instruction. Rather they are ordained by the item writer. There is no point in investigating the processes underlying the responses to the items. After all, nothing can be learned except that comprehension items test comprehension and evaluation items test evaluation, an obvious circularity hardly worth the time to mention. Whatever hierarchical and other transfer relationships exist among these behaviors are entirely determined by the test specialist's theory of those cognitive processes. The only task that seems to remain for the content analyst is to analyze the concept structure of the content and list the items of content, a task perceived as so trivial that neither the content analyst nor the test maker has seen fit to formalize it.

Unfortunately, the psychological theory the test writer imposes in this way is logically inappropriate. First, it effectively obscures the fact that different items of content require the use of different cognitive processes. For example, it would be very difficult to make a convincing argument that the questions *Who rode hard all day?* and *What did the boy do all day?* which were derived from the sentence *The boy rode hard all day* both test identical processes when it is obvious that one item tests the subject of the sentence while the other tests the verb phrase. Yet traditional item-writing theory lumps all such questions into a single cognitive-content category called *sentence comprehension*. Second, the test writer's psychological theory ignores the fact that the instruction does provide instruction in complex cognitive processes. This fact is made more obvious if one tries to imagine how instruction would be carried out if the instruction really did not teach complex cognitive processes. The instruction would probably involve, first, the student's memorizing a long list of sentences which state the factual content, and, second, answering a long list of questions in a trial-and-error fashion until he hits upon the correct cognitive processes required to answer these questions. It seems much more reasonable to argue that the inductive, deductive, expository, and narrative patterns contained in the materials provide the instruction in the very complex cognitive behaviors, while the testlike tasks in the exercises merely force the student to practice those behaviors.

Further, the psychological theory the test writer has imposed on the analysis of instruction is unproductive in the sense that it is a scientific dead end. The cognitive processes the test writers identify are entirely products of their own introspection. At no time have they shown, by appealing to evidence outside their own introspections, that such cognitive processes exist. This would not be fatal, of course, if the theories were verifiable, but they are not. It has already been pointed out that the test writer's categories of items are too poorly defined to permit the rigorously replicable studies required, and it has also been pointed out that the precision of those definitions cannot possibly be sufficiently corrected, because they rest ultimately upon introspection. What can now be added is that the research would be necessarily circular. The processes are defined subjectively by the test writer, who then develops items which represent his subjective concepts. So after the items are studied, all we can say of what has been found is that the items still test whatever the test writer says they test, but we can never prove that the items really test some process different from the one the test writer claims, because his items are the only representation we have of the process he has conceptualized.

On the other hand, the operational approach to item writing does not cause an inversion of the logic of the content-analysis procedure. To define test items for an area of content, it is necessary first to have a theory of the items of content in that area and of their structure. The test items are merely derivations of that theory, since their definitions are constructed from the theory of content developed by the analyst.

Nor does the operational approach impose a psychological theory upon the content analyst. It is based upon the assumption that, if a cognitive process is taught by the instruction, the instruction will take on a discernible pattern or structure. It is these structures which then provide the basis for defining classes of items, and the definitions which result will automatically derive the same classes of items from any instruction exhibiting that structure. But this theory of item writing

31

stands mute on the question what cognitive process a class of items tests. This is regarded as a psychological question which must be appealed to theory built on observed behavior. The psychological theory so developed is, in fact, a statement of the hierarchical and other transfer relationships existing among the items of content in an area of instruction and represents the final objective of the content analyst.

SUMMARY

The purpose of this chapter was to contrast the operational and traditional approaches to item writing in order to show that the traditional methods must be abandoned and replaced by the operational approach. In the traditional approach the test writer outlines the content of instruction and the cognitive behaviors he thinks the students should use to exhibit their mastery of the content. Then, relying on his introspections and those of a panel of advisors, the writer attempts to write a test item which tests each item of content with items in which the item of content is exhibited by each cognitive process. In the operational approach the writer derives the items by first analyzing and labeling the structures underlying the instruction and then by rearranging the instruction to derive the items. The item definition explicitly describes each of the steps in this process.

Four major contrasts between these procedures account for the superiority of the operational approach. First, the traditional approach allows the test writer many options for phrasing items and thus permits his idiosyncrasies to influence scores on the tests; while the operational approach permits the writer no options. Second, the labels attached to traditionally produced items make explicit claims about the cognitive processes underlying the responses to the items; while operationally defined items stand mute on this matter—it is viewed as the proper subject for theory grounded in the observation of behavior. Third, in the traditional procedure the test writer may choose whether or not to write an item, and again his idiosyncrasies are permitted to influence scores on the tests; while in the operational approach the item definitions require the production of all the items possible, and thus item-selection criteria are permitted and required to be rationalized separately. Fourth, in the traditional procedure there is no way to establish the exact feature and segment of the instruction tested by an item, and so no way to define the items of content relevant to a test item and to provide a theory for expecting the instruction to cause the response to the item; while in the operational approach the item's relevance is completely specified.

Because of the flaws inherent in traditional item-writing procedures, tests made from these items are not suitable for use in the major tasks to which achievement tests are put—criterion reference evaluations of a student's mastery of content, instructional programming and other formative-evaluation studies, summative-evaluation studies of both the horse race and time-trial types, and standardized achievement tests for norm referencing a student's performance. Nor can the items constituting these tests serve as the dependent variable in studies in instructional theory or serve to operationalize the content in instructional-content analysis studies. Items made by the operational approach are suitable for use in tests employed for each of these tasks.

The operational approach seems to provide the additional benefit of enabling the test writer to define and count the items of content in a program and thereby to provide a basis for assessing a program's merits in terms of items of content learned per dollar of cost expended.

Construction of
Achievement Test Items

3

REQUIREMENTS OF ITEM TRANSFORMATIONS

A test item can be said to be relevant to instruction only if the item and its correct response can be derived from a specifiable segment of the instruction by using a set of operations which can be both generalized across instructional programs and described in objective terms. A careful analysis of what is meant when it is said that an item is relevant to instruction reveals that an item must correspond in some way to a segment[1] of the instruction, that the response must also correspond in some way to the same segment, and that this segment of instruction must both contain the response and in some way restrict it so that it can occur as the answer to the question. What is being asserted here is that these correspondences can be described in objective terms and that when this is done the descriptions are sufficient to define the relevance of the test item to the instruction.

The restriction that the operations must be generalizable across instructional programs excludes ad hoc descriptions such as could be obtained by simply naming a program and then listing a set of items. Items must be derived by operations which refer to attributes common to the instructional programs of a domain. For example, in mathematics instruction operations might refer to the manipulations performed on the syntactic attributes of mathematical sentences such as $28 + 31 = 59$ to obtain items such as $28 + 31 = \underline{\ ?\ }$ or $59 - 31 = \underline{\ ?\ }$. Hively et al. (1968) have demonstrated such definitions. Or, in the domain of instruction carried on in natural language, the definitions might refer to operations like those by which the syntactic attributes of the sentence

---

1. A segment may be of any size, ranging from a word through the entire instructional program. The word *segment* is used because it refers to an entity having identifiable bounds, a logical necessity for this argument.

The boy rode the horse are operated upon to transform it into the question *Who rode the horse?* Operations such as these are generalizable across programs within their domains, the domains being defined by the different symbol systems by which knowledge is represented.

But to generate tests which are useful for evaluating instructional programs, programming instruction, making criterion reference tests, defining language comprehension instruction, and so on, the operations must also be capable of defining populations of items. To be specific, a given set of operations should be capable of being systematically applied to an instructional program in such a way that all the items of the type derivable by those operations will be produced. When this requirement is met by a set of operations, not only does it insure the definability of item populations but it also insures that tests made by these operations will be independently reproducible given only a knowledge of what operations were used to derive the items and their responses. It also makes it possible to study the properties of classes of items independent of the specific properties of a particular instructional program.

Coining a term, we shall henceforth refer to the operations by which questions and their responses are derived from instruction as *item transformations*. When linguists use the term *transformation* in its general sense, they refer to operations which can be performed on the deep structures underlying language to produce natural language sentences having specified relationships to the original deep structure. As the term item transformation is used here, it has a somewhat analogous meaning except that the sentences and the phrase structures may also be symbolic systems other than natural languages, say, mathematical sentences. Explicitly, the transformations suitable for theoretical linguistics are useful analogies, but they are not identical to those which are most useful in item-writing theory.[2]

ITEM TRANSFORMATIONS

Given the specifications which definitions of item transformations must meet, we can now turn our attention to several sets of transformations which have been developed. What follows is a demonstration of how test items and their responses may be derived from instruction, and the discussion centers largely on transformations which are applicable to instruction in natural language. What is being offered should not be thought of as a set of transformations which can completely define all possible items derivable from natural language; that goal can

---

2. The term *item transformation* is used to distinguish between the procedures defined in theoretical linguistics and the procedures defined in test-item theory.

be reached only after long and arduous research involving the efforts of many persons. At most, the present study should be regarded as only a start toward that goal.

Two cautions must be inserted at this point. Although the subsequent discussion leans heavily upon descriptive devices used in linguistics, this must not be mistaken for a study in linguistic theory. It is a study in item-writing theory. The principal goal of linguistic theory is to represent the linguistic competence of speakers of natural language. The research in item writing seeks general rules with which to fully describe the relationships among test items, their responses, and the instruction. As a result, although some of the same terms and descriptive devices used here are also used in linguistic theory, one should not assume that they refer to identical concepts. A second point must also be understood. Although item-writing theory may lean heavily upon the descriptive devices used in linguistics, it must not be thought that the use of any particular device in item-writing theory implies that a particular linguistic theory is being either accepted or rejected.

Linguistic Description Devices

So that the reader will understand the item transformations to be discussed, a few of the concepts from generative transformational grammar will be introduced. To reduce the amount of space devoted to this introduction, many concepts not absolutely essential have been omitted, as well as some of the more obvious or less important details of the transformations—for example, the *flip-flop* and *do* transformations. Further simplification was achieved by stating the transformations in terms of written English and by using the sentences themselves instead of the symbols representing the underlying structures to demonstrate the arguments. But this should caution the reader that the transformations presented must be thoroughly specified before they can be rigorously applied. For more detailed treatments of syntax, the reader should refer to authors such as Jacobs and Rosenbaum (1967), Thomas (1965), Bach (1964), and Chomsky (1965). Novices should read them in that order.

A grammar is conceived as being a set of abstract symbols and the statements relating those symbols. Figure 1 shows a miniature grammar. Grammars of this sort are actually specialized algebras, and, like other algebras, they can be used to derive theorems. One type of theorem that can be deducted is a sentence. Figure 2 shows an example of a sentence derived, or generated, from the miniature grammar. To make explicit the source of every symbol in each line, just one rule may be applied

$S \rightarrow NP + VP$
$NP \rightarrow D + N$
$VP \rightarrow V + NP$
$D \rightarrow$ the, a, this, that, etc.
$N \rightarrow$ youth, steed, man, house, etc.
$V \rightarrow$ rode, made, saw, took, found, etc.
Where:
S = sentence
NP = noun phrase
$+$ = concatenation symbol
VP = verb phrase
$\rightarrow$ = contains
D = determiner

Fig. 1. A miniature grammar

0. S
1. $NP + VP$
2. $\underline{D + N} + VP$
3. $D + N + \underline{V + NP}$
4. $D + N + V + \underline{D + N}$
5. $\underline{The} + N + V + D + N$
6. The $+ \underline{youth} + V + D + N$
7. The $+$ youth $+ \underline{rode} + D + N$
8. The $+$ youth $+$ rode $+ \underline{the} + N$
9. The $+$ youth $+$ rode $+$ the $+ \underline{steed}$.

Fig. 2. Sentence derived using the miniature grammar

at each step. For example, in step 2 just the $D + N$ was derived, to show that their source was the left-most NP of step 1.

Grammatical theory is stated entirely as a deductive process which starts with an abstract symbol from which a physical representation is derived. It is equally possible to start with a sentence and generate its phrase structure. The latter process has been highly developed as a linguistic research technique with the result that phrase structures can be assigned to sentences to arrive at descriptions like those produced by transformational-generative grammars.

The generation of a sentence can also be represented using what is referred to as a *phrase structure* or a *tree* diagram. Figure 3 shows the tree diagram of the sentence whose generation was shown in figure 2.

Much of the terminology of item transformation refers to tree diagrams. Each letter symbol, such as *S, NP,* or *D,* is called a *node.* Nodes are classified as *terminal* nodes if they are rewritten as words, and they are classified as *nonterminal* nodes if they are rewritten as other nodes.

37

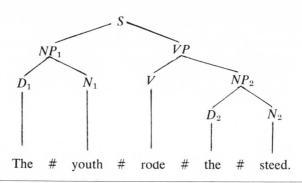

The # youth # rode # the # steed.

Fig. 3. Tree diagram of a sentence

The rewriting takes places from top to bottom in the diagram. Also, nodes may be crudely classified as either *structure* or *lexical* nodes. Roughly speaking, structure nodes carry the labels of classes of words such as articles, conjunctions, auxiliary verbs, prepositions, and so on, while lexical nodes carry the labels of nouns, verbs, adjectives, adverbs, or of phrases including those nodes. A *branch* is a line leading downward from a node, and it may be further designated as *left, right,* or occasionally as *middle* when more than one branch exists. A node is said to *dominate* other nodes if the other nodes are below that node in the tree structure and if those other nodes are connected to it by branches. A *terminal structure* or *terminal string* refers to the terminal nodes of a tree taken as an ordered set.

For the purposes of test-item theory (though not in linguistic theory) a transformation may be regarded as a set of operations which applies to terminal strings to change them into new terminal strings. Some transformations permute the elements in a terminal string and others insert new elements into terminal strings. Figure 4 shows examples of a passive transformation which both permutes elements, as seen in the switching of the positions of the NP_1 and the NP_2, and inserts elements, as seen in the insertions of the auxiliary and the preposition.[3]

$NP_1 - V - NP_2$	$\Rightarrow NP_2 -$ be $-$ en $- V -$ by $- NP_1$
The youth rode the steed.	$\Rightarrow$ The steed was ridden by the youth.
Some boys found the dog.	$\Rightarrow$ The dog was found by some boys.
Hens lay eggs.	$\Rightarrow$ Eggs are laid by hens.

Fig. 4. Passive transformation

3. In linguistic theory the preposition is regarded as existing in the deep structure and not regarded as an inserted element.

In addition, some transformations delete elements from a structure while still others embed one structure into another structure. Figure 5

$D - N_1 - VP \quad D - N_1 - \text{be} - Aj \quad \Rightarrow D - Aj - N_1 - VP$

The boys played ball. The boys were small. ⟹ The small boys played ball.
The old man sat there. He was tired.   ⟹ The tired old man sat there.
The dog barked. The dog was very fierce. ⟹ The very fierce dog barked.

Fig. 5. Transformations involving embeddings

NOTE: The rule shown here is actually a gross oversimplification of what is actually several rules. It is offered here merely to illustrate the notion of embedding.

shows an *embedding* transformation which both deletes elements (the entire subject and verb of the second sentence) and embeds elements from one string into another string (the adjective of the second sentence). The rule shown actually consists of several rules. It is a gross oversimplification presented merely for illustrative purposes.

SENTENCE-DERIVED ITEMS

We can define four kinds of transformations which produce items. Actually there are others, but these will suffice to demonstrate the properties and uses of item transformations. The first three are of secondary interest in testing because they require only the binary response of yes or no and because they test the truth value of the entire sentence rather than test the individual units of information within a sentence. Items of this type will be called *sentence-verification* items.

The first of the sentence-verification items we will call the *echo* item.

$S - . \qquad\qquad \Rightarrow S - ?$

The boy rode the horse. ⟹ The boy rode the horse?
The apples were green. ⟹ The apples were green?

Fig. 6. Echo question

NOTE: Since these item transformations are stated in terms of written English, punctuation instead of intonation will be indicated when it seems necessary for clarity.

Figure 6 shows how a test writer can derive it. This transformation[4] consists of two steps: (*a*) Delete the period at the end of the sentence. (*b*) Insert a question mark at the end of the sentence.

4. Hereinafter the terms *transformation* and *item transformation* will refer to the operations performed by the test writer and not to the concept as it is used in theoretical linguistics. The term *linguistic transformation* will be used to designate the latter.

The echo item might be said to be similar to the items obtained by the practice of taking sentences from a text and presenting them as true-false items. The standard true-false item, however, is preceded by a test instruction rather than followed by a question mark. Representing this practice as a transformation is a simple two-step operation of prefixing a sentence by inserting a specified instruction before the sentence and then stating another rule which permits the test writer who has a series of items of the same type to delete all the instructions except the one associated with the first sentence and to pluralize the noun and verb of that instruction. For example, the instruction for each sentence might read *Mark this sentence true or false*. When all but the first sentence's instructions are deleted, its instructions would be *Mark these sentences true or false*.

We will call the second sentence-verification item the *tag*. Figure 7

$NP_1 - Aux - V - X -$.	$\Rightarrow NP_1 - Aux - V - X -$, $- Aux - Neg - NP_1 -$?
The boy is working.	$\Rightarrow$ The boy is working, isn't he?
The guests have eaten.	$\Rightarrow$ The guests have eaten, haven't they?
The boy should play ball.	$\Rightarrow$ The boy should play ball, shouldn't he?
Where no auxiliary is present:	
$NP_1 - V - X -$.	$\Rightarrow NP_1 - V - X -$, $- do - Neg - NP_1 -$?
The boy worked.	$\Rightarrow$ The boy worked, didn't he?
The guests eat.	$\Rightarrow$ The guests eat, don't they?
The boy plays ball.	$\Rightarrow$ The boy plays ball, doesn't he?
Where a negative is present:	
$NP_1 - Aux - Neg - V - X -$.	$\Rightarrow NP_1 - Aux - Neg - V - X -$, $- Aux - NP_1 -$?
The boy is not working.	$\Rightarrow$ The boy is not working, is he?
The guests haven't eaten.	$\Rightarrow$ The guests haven't eaten, have they?
The boy should not play ball.	$\Rightarrow$ The boy should not play ball, should he?

Fig. 7. Tag items

shows examples of tag items. To derive these questions the test writer performs the following steps, in the order given: (a) deletes the period at the end of the sentence; (b) inserts a comma at the end of the sentence; (c) when the main verb is just a copula or has an auxiliary, repeats the auxiliary or the copula or the word *have* after the comma; (d) when the main verb is not just a copula or has no auxiliary, inserts after the comma the form of the verb *do* which agrees with both the sentence subject and the main verb; (*e*) when the sentence does not contain a negative, inserts a negative suffix to the auxiliary or copula at the end of the sentence; (*f*) inserts at the end of the sentence a copy of the noun phrase such as a pronoun; (*g*) inserts a question mark at the end of the sentence.

Hereinafter, steps referring to punctuation will be omitted from the text.

Figure 8 shows examples of the third sentence-verification item, the

---

When an auxiliary verb is present:

$NP - Aux - V - X - . \Rightarrow Aux - NP - V - X - ?$

The boy is working. $\Rightarrow$ Is the boy working?
The guests have eaten. $\Rightarrow$ Have the guests eaten?
The boy should play ball. $\Rightarrow$ Should the boy play ball?

When only a linking verb is present:

$NP - be - X - . \Rightarrow Be - NP - X - ?$

The weather is warm. $\Rightarrow$ Is the weather warm?
The guests are satiated. $\Rightarrow$ Are the guests satiated?
Bill is President. $\Rightarrow$ Is Bill President?

Where no auxiliary verb is present:

$NP - V - X - . \Rightarrow Do - NP - V - X - ?$

The boy works. $\Rightarrow$ Does the boy work?
The guests ate. $\Rightarrow$ Did the guests eat?
The boy plays ball. $\Rightarrow$ Does the boy play ball?

Fig. 8. Yes/no items

yes/no item. Its two principal operations consist in (*a*) shifting the copula or the auxiliary to the front of the sentence when the main verb consists of just a copula or has an auxiliary; and (*b*) inserting at the front of the sentence a form of the verb *do* when the main verb is not a copula or has no auxiliary.

Using the sentence-verification transformations as described will always produce questions answerable with the response *yes* or *true*. This makes most of the questions in a test true, since instruction, at least ostensibly, contains true references. However, testing considerations require a mixture of true and false questions. Three possibilities arise. The simplest operation to define consists in first applying negative transformations to some specified proportion, say 50 percent, of the deep structures of the sentences sampled for the test; then applying the question transformation. This solution presents a problem. Since most instruction is made up of sentences containing few negatives, and since the chief method of obtaining false sentences would be inserting negatives such as *not* or *un-,* item-response studies would probably show that students quickly develop a response set to mark *false* all questions containing negatives. A second solution might be to restrict the sampling in such a way that half the sentences drawn contain negatives and then to define an operation that alters the negative-affirmative status of a randomly selected half of the sentences.

The third solution cannot be fully defined until the subject of anaphora has been discussed, but it takes this general form: Select randomly the sentences to be tested and then for a random half of these sentences select paired sentences. The paired sentence is selected both because it has a constituent similar in syntactic function to one of the constituents in the first sentence and because none of the constituents of the two sentences have identical referents (where referential identity is determined by the system of reference used in the instruction). In figure 9 the first sentence contains a locative adverbial and is paired

---

a. First Sentence: The boy rode *on the horse.*
b. Second Sentence: There is a flaw *in this procedure.*
c. Derived Sentence: The boy rode in this procedure.
d. Item Transformation: Did the boy ride in this procedure?

Fig. 9. Formation of incorrect yes/no questions

with the second sentence because it contains a constituent, *in this procedure,* having the same syntactic function as the locative adverbial; and because (though it is not demonstrable in this context) none of the constituents of the two sentences share the same referent. The elements identical in syntactic function are then switched from one sentence to the other (the second sentence may either be discarded or kept) to produce the derived sentence. The question (item transformation) which is then derived from the altered sentence is then false relative to the instruction, provided the derived sentence on which the question is based does not happen to occur in the instruction.

Item-response studies would undoubtedly show that many questions produced in this way can be answered correctly without reference to the accompanying instruction (the one in figure 9 is an example) because they describe highly improbable situations. Questions of this kind can be defined and thereby separated from those which have more desirable properties. Lexical words and phrases can, on the basis of restrictions in their co-occurrence with other words, be classified by what are called their *selectional features,* for example, human-nonhuman, animate-inanimate, and abstract-concrete. In nonfigurative speech, words are combined to form sentences in such a way that a head and its modifier (subject and verb, verb and object, etc.) must in certain respects be in agreement with respect to their selectional features. If the procedure outlined above were amended so that the constituents in the paired sentences also matched with respect to subcategorical selectional features, the questions produced would have much less likelihood of being answerable without reference to the instruction.

The so-called wh- item transformation produces questions which are of special interest because of the particular combination of properties possessed by wh- items. Wh- items can question separately every major and lexical node in a sentence. This property is highly desirable, since semantic (as opposed to grammatical) information is signaled at each of the points in a sentence where a modification occurs, and semantic modifications occur primarily at the lexical nodes. Wh- items have the advantage that they can be used for making either multiple-choice or constructed-response items on which the probability of guessing the correct answer is lower than on true-false items. The multiple-choice format offers the still further advantage of allowing the manipulation of the discriminations on which students are tested.

The item transformations for deriving wh- items are somewhat more complex than the ones for deriving sentence-verification items. First consider the simpler ones, the wh- transformations which apply to the subjects of sentences. The test writer performs these operations: (*a*) assigns a structure to the sentence; (*b*) selects the node to be tested using some random or systematic scheme for selecting the node; (*c*) deletes all the words dominated by the node; (*d*) replaces the deleted words with a pro element; and then (*e*) shifts the pro element to the front of the sentence. Figure 10 shows examples of this procedure.

Noun and Noun Phrase Deletion

a. *Joe* hit the ball. $\Rightarrow$ (Who) hit the ball?
b. *The small boy* hit the ball. $\Rightarrow$ (Who) hit the ball?
c. *The small boy who wore a hat* $\Rightarrow$ (Who) hit the ball?
   hit the ball.

Noun Modifier Deletions

d. The *small* boy hit the ball. $\Rightarrow$ (Which) boy hit the ball?
e. The small boy *who wore a hat* $\Rightarrow$ (Which) small boy hit the ball?
   hit the ball.

Fig. 10. Wh- item transformations applying to sentence subjects

The italic print shows the phrase questioned, and the parentheses indicate the pro element substituted for or proing the phrase questioned.

There are four groups of pro elements. *Who* and *what* are used to replace human and nonhuman nouns, respectively; the word *which* is used to pro noun modifiers; the pro elements *how, when, where,* and *why* pro the various categories of adverbials. The pro elements replacing verbs are a bit more complicated. When the verb itself is deleted, it is replaced by the phrase *what do.* But when the pro element and its auxiliary are shifted to the front of the sentence, only the word *what* is shifted, and the *do* is left in place.

The steps for making deletions in the predicate of a sentence are identical to those for making deletions in the subject for steps (*a*) through (*d*). Figure 11 shows the results of applying the rules for

---

Noun and Noun Phrase Deletions

   a. Joe hit *the ball.* $\Rightarrow$ (What did) Joe hit?
   b. Joe hit the *round ball.* $\Rightarrow$ (What did) Joe hit?

Noun Modifier Deletions

   c. Joe hit the *round* ball. $\Rightarrow$ (Which) ball (did) Joe hit?
   d. Joe hit the ball *we gave him.* $\Rightarrow$ (Which) ball (did) Joe hit?

Adverbial Deletions

   e. Joe hit the ball *hard.* $\Rightarrow$ (How did) Joe hit the ball?
   f. Joe hit the ball *this morning.* $\Rightarrow$ (When did) Joe hit the ball?
   g. Joe hit the ball *over the fence.* $\Rightarrow$ (Where did) Joe hit the ball?
   h. Joe hit the ball *to get on base.* $\Rightarrow$ (Why did) Joe hit the ball?

Fig. 11. Wh- item transformations applying to sentence predicates

making deletions in the predicate. In step (*e*) the appropriate form of the verb *do* is inserted (the form of the main verb is altered if necessary) if the main verb does not have an auxiliary; in step (*f*) the auxiliary is shifted to the front of the sentence; in step (*g*) the noun is shifted to the front of the sentence if the deleted element modified a noun; and finally, in step (*h*) the pro element is shifted to the front of the sentence.

It should be noted that this description (as do all the others) still leaves some of the details of the wh- item transformation unspecified.

It is possible to define several different populations of responses to wh- questions, but only two can be defined before anaphora, synonym substitution, and paraphrase transformations have been discussed. The most obvious scoring rule is to accept as correct just those responses which exactly duplicate the words deleted from the sentence in order to make the question. This rule must be augmented greatly before it is possible to define rigorously all the responses which can be reasonably regarded as correct responses to wh- items.

Presenting wh- items in a multiple-choice format introduces the interesting problem of how the population of response distractors can be defined for an item. One possibility is to make a list consisting of all the constituents occurring in the instruction which have the same syntactic and selectional features as the phrase deleted to form the question but which do not have the same referent as the deleted phrase. The distractors for an item can then be randomly sampled from this list. Several other possibilities will be suggested in connection with the descriptive devices still to be introduced.

But the item transformations, both the wh- and the sentence-verification types, are sufficient to define only a small part of the items which can be derived from sentences. Consider the four questions and the four responses in figure 12. Only question (*a*) and response (*a*) can

---

Base Sentence: The diminutive youth mounted the steed.

Questions	Responses
a. Who mounted the steed?	*a.* The diminutive youth
b. By whom was the steed mounted?	*b.* The youth who was diminutive
c. Who climbed on the horse?	*c.* The small young man
d. By whom was the horse climbed on?	*d.* The young man who was small

---

Fig. 12. Some additional item types

be derived from the base sentence using just the descriptive devices presented up to this point. This is true even though the questions seemingly require about the same knowledge to answer, and the answers each seem to represent that knowledge fairly well.

To define questions and responses of these types it is necessary to introduce two additional descriptive devices which we will call the *paraphrase transformation* and the *semantic substitute*.[5] And, to keep the discussion ordered, it is also necessary to define four categories of items: the *rote* item, the *transform* item, the *semantic-substitute* item, and the *compound* item. Rote items are items of the type just described. What identifies them as rote items is the fact that they are derived directly from the base sentence (the sentence in exactly the form in which it appears in the instruction) without first in some way altering the base sentence.

The transform item is derived by first performing a paraphrase transformation on the base sentence appearing in the instruction and then applying item transformations to the derived sentences. A paraphrase transformation operates on one of the sentences in the instruction, hereinafter called the *base sentence,* to produce a new sentence, hereinafter called the *derived sentence,* which has a somewhat different

---

5. Neither the paraphrase nor the semantic-substitute device is used in theoretical linguistics. Their introduction here should serve as another illustration of the lack of identity between theoretical linguistics and item writing theory.

form but essentially the same meaning as the base sentence. Figure 13 gives examples of four paraphrase transformations and shows the rote and transform questions corresponding to each. Notice that in every case both the rote and the transform question test the same node in the phrase-structure tree of the base sentence. This illustration shows only

Base:	The small boy rode.	R*	Which boy rode?
Derived:	The boy was small. The boy rode.	T*	What was the boy?**
Base:	The boy was small.	R	Who was small?
Derived:	It was the boy who was small.	T	Who was it who was small?
Base:	The boy who was small rode.	R	Which boy rode?
Derived:	The boy was small. The boy rode.	T	What was the boy?**
Base:	The boy rode the horse.	R	Who rode the horse?
Derived:	The horse was ridden by the boy.	T	By whom was the horse ridden?

Fig. 13. Some paraphrase transformations

* R = rote question; T = transform question.

** It is unlikely that anyone would answer this question with the response *small*. In actual practice test writers test this kind of structure using what I call a *semantically cued* question such as "How large was the boy?" These questions are formed by inserting a semantic substitute of the deleted form, along with the pro word, into the slot left by the deletion.

a few of the many paraphrase transformations. Menzel (see Appendix) has provided what seems to be the most comprehensive survey available of the paraphrase transformations used in English. Although only wh- items are illustrated in figure 13, any item transformation can be applied to the derived sentences.

The paraphrase transformation as a device for defining items makes an enormous contribution to our ability to give precise definitions to items. Figure 14 shows just a few of the questions which can be derived

Base: A very old man who lives up the street led his dog up to a store window one day.

Who led his dog?	Who lives up the street?
What did the man do?	When was his dog led?
What did the man lead?	Whose dog was led?
When did the man lead his dog?	To which window was his dog led?
How old was the man?	Who lives up the streeet?
By whom was the dog led?	Where was his dog led?
Who was very old?	What was led?
Which man led his dog?	What was led up to a window?
Where does the man live?	What was the window in?

Fig. 14. Some transform items derived from a sentence

from base sentences using paraphrase transformations. Without the paraphrase question none of these questions could be defined in any reasonably efficient way. It should also be clear that the paraphrase transformation has its analogue in algebras other than those used to describe the syntax of natural language. For example, given the sentence $8 + 7 = 15$, we can derive the transform question $(2 \times 4) + 7 = \underline{?}$

The use of the paraphrase transformation also makes it possible to define additional correct responses to wh- questions. Figure 15 shows

---

Base: The small boy who wore a hat hit the ball.
Rote Item: Who hit the ball? (The small boy who wore a hat)

Transform Responses

a. The small boy	*e.* The one who wore a hat
b. The boy who wore a hat	*f.* The one wearing a hat
c. The boy	*g.* It was the small boy.
d. The one who was small	*h.* It was the boy.

Fig. 15. Transform responses

a base sentence, a rote item, and then a series of transform responses to the rote question. None of these responses could be easily defined without the paraphrase transformation.

The introduction of the paraphrase transformation also makes it possible to enlarge the size of the population from which multiple-choice distractors are selected. Without the paraphrase transformation it was possible to use a phrase as a distractor only if it performed precisely the same syntactic function as the phrase which was deleted to form the question. There is a class of paraphrase transformations which describe how a phrase which performs a given function may be transformed so that it can perform a different syntactic function. Consider the verb phrase in *He ate the apples*. It can be transformed into a noun phrase as in *His eating of the apples made him sick*. This class of transformations makes it possible to include as distractors phrases which meet all the other criteria except that they do not conform to the proper part of speech category.

Semantic-substitute items are derived by substituting synonyms for one or more of the lexical words or phrases in the base sentence and then applying question transformations to the derived sentence. Figure 16 shows an example of this procedure. But before semantic-substitute items can be defined rigorously, the synonym itself must be given a rigorous definition, which is no small task since semantics is one of the less explored areas of linguistics. However, it seems possible to develop definitions of synonymity having a degree of objective reproducibility sufficient to serve the highly specialized needs of testing. What follows

Base:	The diminutive youth mounted the steed.	
Derived:	The small young man climbed on the horse.	

Questions	Responses
a. Who climbed on the horse?	The small young man . . .
b. Which young man climbed on the horse?	The small . . .
c. Which small man climbed on the horse?	The young . . .
d. What did the small young man do?	Climbed on the horse . . .
e. What did the small young man climb on?	The horse . . .

Fig. 16. Derivation of semantic-substitute items

should be regarded as a tentative suggestion of the form those definitions might take.

First, it seems necessary to distinguish two formal types of synonyms, the *lexical* and the *phrasal synonyms.* Lexical synonyms are single words such as *wide* and *broad, tall* and *high,* and *heavy* and *weighty* which stand (at least in some contexts) in some synonymity relationship to each other. Phrasal synonyms consist of pairs the members of which stand in some synonymity relationship to each other but in which one or both members consist of a phrase, clause, or some more complex syntactic unit.

Second, it is necessary to distinguish between *symmetrically* and *hierarchically related synonyms.* Symmetrically related synonyms are pairs the members of which have nearly identical referents when they appear in a specified context. For example, the words *wide* and *broad* seem to be such a pair when they occur in the context *wide stream* and *broad stream.* What distinguishes them as symmetrically related is the fact that they can be inserted in the first frame in figure 17 without

Symmetrical:	The set of all X *(things)* are included in the set of all Y *(things)* and the set of all Y *(things)* are included in the set of all X *(things).*
Hierarchical:	The set of all X *(things)* are included in the set of all Y *(things)* but the set of all Y *(things)* are not included in the set of all X *(things).*

Fig. 17. Frames for testing synonymity relationships

making that sentence false. Hierarchically related synonyms do not have identical referents when they are substituted in the same context. Rather one member, the *including term,* refers to a set which includes the set referred to by the other member, the *included term.* What distinguishes them as hierarchically related synonyms is the fact that they can be inserted into the second frame in figure 17 without making that sentence false. Synonym sets are not limited to pairs but may consist of sets of any size, as in hierarchical chains such as *Mable, angora, cat, feline, mammal, vertebrae, animal,* and *living being.* Obviously, the synonymity of terms can be determined only with respect to a specific context.

Symmetrically related synonyms can be substituted for each other in deriving sentences that paraphrase a base sentence. Occasionally, one member of a synonym pair may have to be transformed so that it can function syntactically in the same way as the other. For example, the members *scissors* and *two-bladed cutting instrument* of a synonym pair cannot serve the same function unless suitably transformed. But, when the members of a pair are hierarchically related and suitably transformed, the including term may be substituted for the included term although an included term cannot be substituted into the base sentence for its including synonym. For example, given the base sentence *The house cat climbed the tree,* we can derive *The feline climbed the tree* because the set of all felines includes the set of all house cats; but when we start with the base sentence *The feline climbed the tree* we cannot correctly derive *The house cat climbed the tree* because the set of all felines is not included in the set of all house cats, and therefore the term in the base may have referred to another of its subclasses—tigers, for example.

Semantic-substitute items are defined as questions and responses which are derived, first, by substituting for at least one term in the base sentence either one of its including or symmetrical synonyms and, second, by applying an item transformation to the sentences so derived. The question stem and its response must be classified separately depending on whether any words in that portion of the item can be represented as having been derived by the semantic-substitute procedure. It should also be noted that, whenever a phrasal substitution is made, the question or response in which the phrasal synonym appears must be classed as a compound, the next item type to be defined.

Introducing semantic substitution as a descriptive device also increases the number of populations of distractor phrases for use in making multiple-choice tests. One obvious addition to the distractor populations is obtained from the semantic substitutions of items already on the list. A population of special interest can be obtained by listing for a given correct response all the included and including terms hierarchically synonymous with the rote response. Selecting distractors from chains of this sort would seem to make it possible to systematically study in the context of item-response studies discriminations presently receiving attention only in concept-development research.

Responses in a hierarchical chain of this sort present a problem in the scoring of constructed-response questions. A response must seemingly be scored correct if it has an inclusion relationship with the rote response to the item even if the including response is so general in referent as to be vague and nebulous. This is so because scoring correct only rote and transform responses and their symmetrical substitutes seems too stringent a criterion to be defended; yet there are no readily apparent logical grounds for establishing a point at which an including synonym becomes so general as to be considered wrong.

Compound items are defined as question stems and responses obtained by applying the transform and the semantic-substitute procedures to the base sentence before the question transformations are applied.

Other types of sentence-based items remain to be defined, and the definitions given here need to be systematically catalogued and their operations specified in greater detail. However, the descriptive devices mentioned here seem sufficient to accomplish the task. That is, populations of sentence-based questions can be completely defined and taxonomized by specifying (a) the syntactic nodes tested, (b) the position of those nodes in the deep structure and surface structure of sentences, (c) the operations performed on the base sentences, (d) the item transformation applied, and (e) the operations used to select the response distractors when they are used. This is not to say that additional attributes, such as conceptual categories of responses, cannot also be used to define item populations, provided they are defined rigorously. Rather, it is to say that the form of the item is completely specified when at least these features are specified.

DISCOURSE-DERIVED ITEMS

Much information is signaled by the relationships between sentences. Two phenomena are of interest here, *anaphora* and *intersentence syntax*. Descriptions of each phenomenon provide important devices for defining additional populations of items. It should be pointed out, however, that linguists have done little research into these phenomena, with the result that persons doing research at these levels of item-writing theory must be prepared to do some linguistic research themselves.

Anaphora are pro structures called *anaphoric* expressions which refer back to (or substitute for) some structure called an *antecedent* or *postcedent* which appears in a different clause.[6] Anaphora permit an author

---

6. Anaphora may involve either an antecedent structure as in *When I saw John, he was eating,* or a postcedent structure as in *When I saw him, John was eating.*

to introduce a term, modify it, set the term as modified equal to some short pro structure, and thereafter refer in other sentences to the entire modified concept using just the pro structure.

Figure 18 shows examples of four major types of anaphora. These

---

PRO WORDS

a.	*N**	*Joe* picked up the bat. (He) is a good hitter.**
b.	*V*	Joe *eats ice cream by the gallon.* Jim (does [so]), too.
c.	*Aj*	*Muscular boys* showed up. (This kind [of boy]) plays well.
d.	*Av*	Joe sat *under a tree.* This air was cool (there).
e.	*S*	*Joe may be able to play.* The team hopes (so).

DELETED MODIFIERS

f.	*N*	*The boy with the hat* will pitch. (This boy) is good.
g.	*V*	The boys *practiced hard.* (This [practice]) helped.
h.	*Aj*	Joe was *extremely fast.* (This fast) a player was needed.
i.	*Av*	Joe went *somewhat reluctantly.* (This [reluctance]) was unusual.

ELLIPSIS

j.	*N*	The boys wanted to eat *a quart of ice cream.* There wasn't (that much [. . .] left, so they had to be satisfied with what they got.
k.	*V*	Although I don't *see Bill much these days,* she seems (to [. . .]).
l.	*Aj*	The stands were *green.* The fence was (. . .), too.
m.	*Av*	We all agreed to meet at nine o'clock. The boys were *on time.* The girls were not (. . .).

SEMANTIC SUBSTITUTE

n.	*N*	Jim gathered *the bats and balls.* He put (this equipment) away.
o.	*V*	The boys *played very hard.* (Their effort) won the game.
p.	*Aj*	The boys were *able and eager.* (These qualities) helped.
q.	*Av*	John sat *on the roof.* (This perch) helped him see better.
r.	*S*	*Joe hurt his hand.* (This accident) worried the team.

Fig. 18. Four types of anaphora

* *N* = nominal, *V* = verbal, *Aj* = adjectival,
Av = adverbial, and *S* = sentential.
** Antecedents are italicized and anaphoric elements are in parentheses.

are pro words, deleted modifiers, ellipses, and semantic substitutes. As shown, any lexical item can be involved in an anaphorization. What is not shown is that paragraphs and even larger units can function as antecedents. For example, given a paragraph describing a developing flood condition, one could anaphorize this paragraph by beginning the next paragraph with the phrase *This situation. . . .*

One of the tests used (Menzel, Appendix) to identify anaphoric relationships is also a useful device for deriving anaphora-based items. The test consists of deleting the anaphoric expression and substituting for it its antecedent to see if an accurate paraphrase results. Or, one can put the antecedent and the anaphoric expression on either side of the copula *be* (unless the antecedent is longer than a sentence) and then determine that the resulting sentence is not anomalous. This operation provides the first step in the derivation of anaphora-based items. Figure 19 shows how a test writer would derive an anaphora-based item. The

Base:	Joe sat *under the tree.* The air was cool (there).
Embed:	The air was cool under the tree.
Insert:	The air was cool where?
Permute:	Where was the air cool?

Fig. 19. Derivation of anaphora-based items

steps in this procedure consist of (*a*) deleting the anaphoric expression from the sentence in which it appears, (*b*) embedding in its place the antecedent, (*c*) comparing the antecedent and the anaphoric expression to determine the elements deleted to form the anaphora, (*d*) replacing the deleted element of the anaphoric expression with the appropriate wh- pro element, and (*e*) completing the wh- transformations.

Anaphora-based items are classified as rote, transform and the like on the basis of the operations performed after the antecedent has been embedded. But to define and taxonomize anaphora items it is also necessary to specify the operations involved in the embedding of the antecedent. For example, to embed the antecedent shown in example (*g*) of figure 18, the verb phrase must be nominalized before it can be embedded in the place of the anaphoric expression.

Anaphoric questions can often be shown to have a number of correct answers. Figure 20 shows why this is true. The reason is that anaphora represent the repeated occurrences of a term. Each time the term occurs it may be modified. If the modifiers are nominalized or otherwise transformed they can be set into identity relationships with the term normally considered to be the correct answer to the question. To achieve simplicity, the demonstration offered in figure 20 omits the transformational details, but it can be stated with whatever degree of rigor one chooses with no change in the result.

To return momentarily to the selection of distractors for sentence-based questions for multiple-choice questions, it was specified that the distractors may not share the same referent as the correct response. Referential identity is defined by anaphoric analyses of the type just demonstrated in figure 20. With this amendment added, the rules for defining the populations of distractors for sentence-based questions can also be used for defining the populations of distractors for anaphoric items.

a. Given the text:
Joe picked up the bat. (He) is a good hitter.

b. By anaphoric analysis we get:
He → Joe. (Literally, this reads, He is identical to Joe.)

c. By paraphrase transformation we get:
Joe is the one who picked up the bat. or
Joe → the one who picked up the bat.

d. From step *a* we get:
He → a good hitter.

e. From steps *b, c,* and *d* we obtain:
He → Joe → a good hitter → the one who picked up the bat.

f. Now, given the anaphora question:
Who is a good hitter?

g. We can derive the answers:
Joe and The one who picked up the bat.

h. The phrase "a good hitter" was preempted by the question and the use of personal pronouns as responses is usually ruled out by the test instructions.

Fig. 20. Multiple correct answers for anaphora-based questions

Figure 20 should make it clear that, when the items are derived from connected discourse and when they are in a constructed-response format, it is often impossible to test just the knowledge specific to a sentence. In one study the author and his students constructed twenty-seven rote, sentence-based completion questions, with each question derived from a different passage, and gave them to 100 children enrolled in grade 4. Between 10 and 40 percent of the correct responses to the different questions could be represented as being anaphorically derived.[7]

Information is signaled by the order in which sentences, paragraphs, and larger sections appear relative to each other. Another class of questions, the *intersentence questions,* tests knowledge of this information. To illustrate, the question *What caused the dog to bark and jump?* is likely to elicit one answer if the sentences *The dog jumped and barked* and *The door opened* are presented in that order, and a different answer if they are presented in the order *The door opened* and *The dog jumped and barked.* The relative positions of sentences, paragraphs, and so on, signal causation, sequence in time, subordination, and

7. It is also worth noting that we were able to devise objective rules for scoring the constructed responses. These rules were sufficiently accurate to classify over twenty-seven hundred responses with only about two hundred responses being unclassifiable chiefly because the students had used grammatical forms that were ambiguous. The scoring rules can be used reliably by anyone with a fair background in linguistics.

several other kinds of information. Occasionally, this information is accurately represented by joining segments of discourse with words or phrases like *because* or *for these reasons*. More often the conjunctions are ambiguous—for example, *and, or, then,* and *while*—or no conjunctions at all are used.

Since there has been very little study of these phenomena, there is little knowledge of how the formal features of language correlate with these relationships or, indeed, whether the relationships are structurally signaled at all. However, Menzel (Appendix) has worked out a procedure which may permit these relationships to be replicably identified, and this procedure may, in turn, be used to derive a population of questions. Since this procedure has received only limited testing, it is offered here only for its heuristic value.

Figure 21 shows an example of how items may be derived using this

---

a. Base discourse:
    (A) Joe broke his arm.   (B) He was riding.   (C) He fell off his horse.

b. Nominalize all sentences:
    (A) Joe broke his arm. → The breaking of Joe's arm . . .
    (B) Joe was riding. → Joe's riding . . .
    (C) Joe fell off his horse. → Joe's falling off his horse . . .

c. Test the adjacent sentences in the matrices:
    1. *C* occurred during *B*.
    2. *C–B* caused *A*.

d. Embed nominalizations into the matrices:
    1. Joe's falling off his horse *occurred during* his riding.
    2. Joe's falling off his horse occurring during his riding *caused* the breaking of his arm.

e. Derive questions:
    1*a.* What occurred during Joe's riding?*
    1*b.* When did Joe's falling off his horse occur?
    2*a.* What caused the breaking of Joe's arm?*
    2*b.* What did Joe's falling off his horse occurring during his riding cause? or What was caused by Joe's falling off his horse during his riding?

Fig. 21. Suggested derivation of items based on intersentence syntax

* When a causal or time relationship is being tested using a constructed response item, the correct answers to some of the questions may be any antecedent in the causal or time sequence.

device. The procedure consists of the following general steps: (*a*) Nominalize all sentences. (*b*) Test each sentence pair in the sentence conjunction matrices until a pair is found which can fit one of the matrices and at the same time mantain paraphrase identity with the base text. (*c*) Embed into the sentence-conjunction matrix the sentence pair that fits. (*d*) Nominalize the sentence obtained by the embedding. (*e*) Continue fitting nominalized sentences into the matrices until a single sentence is obtained. (*f*) Form wh- items by deleting one or the other nominalized sentences for each of the sentences derived by the embeddings.

The embedding procedure has the effect of determining a tree structure for the discourse. There seem to be no limits on the size of a segment of discourse included in a single tree.

It is probably too early in this research to attempt to define a population of distractor items, but one interesting fact does emerge. When a question requires the student to state the cause of some event, and the immediate cause is part of a time-conditioned sequence, the student can name any event in that sequence. This, like the hierarchical synonym, suggests the possibility of testing and shaping discriminations between immediate and ultimate or direct and indirect causes.

From the small amount of experience gained with intersentence questions, two observations seem worth noting. First, as questions are formed at higher and higher nodes in the tree structures of the discourse, either the questions or the responses become longer and longer. At the high nodes there is no way to distinguish between the very long responses and the essay responses for the same questions. Second, people (assorted colleagues) seem to place higher subjective values on the knowledge tested by questions testing the higher nodes in the discourse-tree structure. They often describe these questions as *getting at the basic ideas of the instruction* or something similar.

Assumptions and Methods in Item-writing Research

4

It seems necessary to devote some discussion to the methods and assumptions of item-writing research. Although for the moment the anaphora-based question represents the upper bound to which we have carried our definitions for populations of items, this by no means represents the maximum limit attainable. *In principle there is no reason why any item type whatever cannot be operationally defined.* And as a simple matter of fact, achievement testing can produce only meaningless results until the test items presently in use have been rigorously defined. But a great deal of research will be required to reach just this objective, and there is every reason to expect new item types to be invented in the future.

At least four broad categories of activity can be identified in item-writing research: (*a*) selecting or creating the item type to be defined, (*b*) assigning a structure to the instruction, (*c*) assigning a structure to the items, and (*d*) devising rules for relating the structures of the items to the structures of the instruction. The following discussion will explore some of the assumptions and methods employed in this work.

Selecting and Creating Items to be Defined

It should be explicitly recognized that the reason for inventing a particular type of item is that that type of item permits us to observe some class of cognitive behavior of interest to us. It should also be explicitly recognized that the act of inventing the item type is an intuitive, not a mechanical, process. That is, the creation of examples of a new class of items is done entirely subjectively and represents the first step in the definition of the creator's subjective concept of a cognitive behavior involved in learning.

At least for the present, it seems preferable to concentrate item-writing research on defining the types of items already in use rather than upon inventing new types of items. The first reason for this judgment is that, until we have objectively defined the items already in use, it is probably impossible to verify the claim that the item type invented is indeed new. This is because, in the absence of definitions for known item types, it is impossible to distinguish them from newly invented item types. Second, it seems likely that in the course of developing definitions of the types of items already known a number of new item types will be invented as a by-product. Third, any new item type invented is likely to involve complex cognitive processes and to require correspondingly complex descriptive devices in its definition.[1] So it seems likely that attempts to invent a new category at too early a stage would be frustrated by our inability to define the category.

In selecting a category of items to be defined, the investigator should adhere closely to subjective judgments of what constitutes a category of items which test the same cognitive process. To be useful, an item definition should have some psychological significance to the people who use it. It is true that intuition hardly constitutes sufficient evidence that all the items lumped into the same category do indeed test the same process, and it is also true that only experimental analysis can provide the kind of data required for categorizing the items. Yet it is equally true that experimental analyses are operationally meaningless unless the items they study are operationally defined. Intuitive judgments of item similarity provide a necessary theoretical basis for the careful analytic work which follows. The categories can then be changed as the experimental evidence subsequently requires.

ASSIGNING A STRUCTURE TO THE INSTRUCTION

Necessary to all uses of achievement tests is the assumption that there is an abstract structure underlying instruction. In the cases of the item definitions offered here, the abstract structures used were the semantic and syntactic relationships of the language in the instruction. These types of structures have been fairly well worked out at the lower levels of analysis of not only natural language but also mathematics and the other logical languages. Even graphic representation seems to be governed by a definite system of structure rules. To give an example,

---

1. This should not be interpreted as implying in any way that there is a necessary correspondence between the transformations used to define an item and the cognitive processes which underlie a student's response to the item. The two notions must be kept strictly separated. However, at least to the author, there has appeared to be some correlation between his subjective judgment of the complexity of the cognitive processes underlying the response to an item type and the amount of descriptive paraphernalia required to derive that type of item.

the message transmitted by a sequence of pictorial illustrations can be distorted and often reduced to uninterpretable nonsense by a random reshuffling of the order of the illustrations. This fact constitutes sufficient evidence to support the claim that an abstract structure underlies the sequence of illustrations.

While it seems indisputable and even obvious that there is a low-level structure underlying the linguistic forms used in instruction, it may not be immediately obvious that there are a number of higher-level factors which impose constraints upon the structure and content of instruction and which must also be regarded as a part of the abstract structure of instruction. We will briefly identify these, show how each affects the content or structure of instruction, and then show why each must be considered in item-writing theory.

To begin with the most obvious case, the subject matter itself provides the content of instruction. And it is generally recognized that the subject matter provides basic structural constraints for ordering the sequence of content. This is commonly referred to by the term *content structure*. The fundamental principle underlying the organization of the content in any field is hierarchical. That is, the first concept presented is essential for the definition of the second concept, the two concepts are essential for the definition of concepts presented still later, and so on, forming hierarchies of concepts. As a notational convenience, it is possible to represent the structure of a subject matter area as a logico-deductive system in which the most abstract concept appears at the top of the hierarchy and concepts at a second level of abstraction are represented as nodes branching from the most abstract concept. Third-level terms branch from second-level terms, and so on. The terminal nodes in this tree consist of the set of all true statements about that subject matter area. The rules governing this process will hereinafter be called the *content-structure rules*.

The content-structure rules set limits on but do not completely determine the structure of the content of instruction. For example, in physics there is no reason why the mechanical principle of the lever has to be discussed before electricity is introduced. But molecular theory must be introduced before the topic of thermodynamics. So the structure of the content provides important but by no means the only constraints on the structure of instruction.

Gagné (1967) has shown that it is impossible to specify what an item tests unless we take into account the content structure. He begins by pointing out that many of the behaviors we teach have a hierarchical dependence; for example, the capability of solving division problems depends upon the capability of solving mulitplication problems which, in turn, depends upon the capability of solving addition problems. He then points out that this dependence makes a response to an item ambiguous. When the student gives an incorrect answer to a multiplication problem, say, we are not sure whether the response indicates that the student has failed to learn multiplication or whether he has failed to learn one of the component capabilities upon which multiplication depends. Only by testing the component capabilities can this ambiguity be reduced. It follows then that an item response cannot be defined apart from the context of the responses to the other items in the same hierarchy. Therefore, content structure must be incorporated as an essential part of item definitions. These same concepts will also be discussed with respect to item-response theory.

The second factor which constrains the structure of instruction we will call the *psychological rules*. A substantial proportion of the research in instructional psychology has been devoted to attempts to determine the best way to organize instructional statements. To name just a few of the possible examples: some have tried to determine whether example statements should precede or follow rule statements; others have studied the effects of inserting advanced organizers into the instruction; and still others have studied the dimensions along which language varies in difficulty. The net effect of investigations of this general type is that rules are stated which impose contraints upon the structure of the instruction.

The psychological rules influence the manner in which knowledge will be taught and tested. Consider arithmetic instruction, the objective of which is to enable the student to answer every possible arithmetic problem he will encounter. It is at least conceivable that this objective could be attained by simply having him memorize the answers to every possible problem. Instead, the psychological rules select from the content algorithms which are then taught as cognitive behaviors. And these cognitive behaviors permit the student to solve all the problems he encounters. Explicitly, mathematics and other content areas are neutral with respect to instructional strategy. It is in instructional psychology, therefore, that teaching strategies are studied, and consequently it is in the psychological rules that we determine how content will be taught and whether, for example, it will be tested as a paired-associate task or as a complex transfer task. Similar arguments could be advanced to show that the language in the instruction and, therefore, the language in the items are similarly determined in the psychological rules.

The third factor imposing structure upon the instruction might be called the *value rules*. If we set out to teach all the content of an area we would shortly discover ourselves teaching subject matter we judge to be trivial, and we would find that we had preempted our resources for teaching other things we judge to be important. Instead of teaching everything in an area, we apply value judgments to the selection of just that content which maximizes the attainment of our values. Hence, our value systems operate to select or delete content and, therefore, must be regarded as a part of the abstract structure underlying instruction.

The work of Hively et al. (1968) on the universe-defined item has graphically illustrated why the value rules must be considered in the definitions of achievement test items. He defines universes of arithmetic computation problems by devising computational algorithms which generate every possible item of a specified type. For example, he presents one algorithm which produces every subtraction item in which the minuend is less than ten. It is a relatively simple matter to apply this concept to other subject matter areas. We could produce, say, all items in geography testing knowledge of place location. This would produce not only an item testing knowledge of the location of Chicago but also one testing knowledge of the location of Gnaw Bone, Indiana— an item which is not likely to be derived from any major instructional program. By almost any value rules, the location of Gnaw Bone would not be regarded as content of great importance.

This should serve to illustrate the argument that instruction exists in two forms—an exhaustive, or universe, form and a form reduced by the application of value rules. Items derived directly from instruction can always be regarded as testing valued knowledge because the items are relevant to a segment of the instruction and because the values are always (hopefully) applied to the instruction. Conversely, we can imagine some items appearing in a universe-defined set which test knowledge to which very low and perhaps negative values are assigned. Since a test item is meaningless unless it is relevant to (or implies) some instructional content, we are forced to conclude that underlying an instructional program there exists a form of instruction which includes all the content of an area of discourse and that the universe of content was operated upon by the value rules to produce the form of the actual instruction.

The last set of rules to be discussed will be referred to as *redundancy rules*. To explain the existence of items which we think of as measuring the transfer, application, and evaluation capabilities of students, it is first necessary to postulate the existence of the redundancy rules. Once content has been selected as important to teach, we seldom teach every item in that area. Rather, we teach students cognitive behaviors and have them practice these behaviors on a few examples. We do this to enable students to deduct the answers to all the remaining problems of that type. These cognitive behaviors include the so-called thinking or logical behaviors as well as the simpler behaviors found in mathematics, phonics, and the like. Consequently, it is necessary to postulate the existence of a set of redundancy rules which separate the items of content upon which practice is provided from the items of content which can be deducted from those taught. The items derived from the instruction deleted by the redundancy rules, then, include those measuring transfer, application, and evaluation.

What have just been described are what seem to be the major components of the abstract structure underlying instruction. To some it will be self-evident that this structure has been conceptualized as both a deductive system, which generates instruction from a set of given objectives, and an inductive system, which infers an underlying structure and objectives from a given instructional program. The inductive analysis could begin with the test items, provided the items were completely labeled by specifying what transformations were used in their derivation.

Since deductive systems are relatively unfamiliar in the area of measurement and evaluation, a rough description will be given of how the analysis generates an instructional program. The analysis starts with the objectives as given. Actually they are themselves derived by a set of elaborate procedures which can be regarded as irrelevant to the scope of the present discussion.

Starting with an instructional objective, say the teaching of physics, we can apply the content-structure rules to infer that several categories of instruction will be taught—mechanics, molecular mechanics, electricity, and so on. Each of these abstract categories of content can in turn be analyzed into third-level abstractions, the third-level abstractions into fourth-level abstractions, and so on, until the terminal nodes are reached. When the terminal nodes are produced, they contain the set of all true statements about physics along with illustrations and examples of those statements. It should also be noted that the statements are ordered according to their hierarchical structure. Those involving concrete terms appear first, or *on the left,* and progress to statements containing abstract terms on the right.

Next, the value rules are applied to select just that content which maximizes the values given. The psychological rules are applied to further sequence the instruction and to cast it into suitable natural language. Then the redundancy rules are applied to separate from the content actually to be presented the content which can be deducted from that presented. Finally, the item-derivation rules can be applied.

Several important benefits are gained by assigning an explicit structure to instructional programs. First, many populations of items cannot be defined at all unless a structure is assigned. For example, it is impossible to define a transfer item unless we postulate a set of instructional statements deleted by a set of redundancy rules. Thus, the question *What color was the house* would constitute a transfer item if the instruction contained as the only relevant sentence *The house blended with the summer foliage.* And the only way to define that question is through the application of a set of redundancy rules which permit us to recover the deleted sentence *The house was green.* Another example is furnished by Hively's universe-defined items, which may be defined only if we assume that they are derived from instruction generated without applying the value rules.

The second major advantage is of considerable importance. Scriven (1967) showed that it is impossible to attach a value to (i.e., to evaluate) a response to an item which is considered in isolation. He argued that we attach values to objectives and that unless an item's relevance to an objective can be demonstrated no value can be attached to the item. It should be noted that in the same discussion Scriven claimed that demonstrating an item's relevance to an objective and demonstrating its relevance to the instruction are different and independent processes. This is incorrect, for the item must be traced through the instruction before we can say what objective it tests. To return to an earlier illustration, the question *What color was the house?* would be assigned one value if the instruction contained as the only relevant sentence *The house was green,* and quite a different value if the instruction contained only the sentence *The house blended with the summer foliage.* Thus, an item's relevance can be determined only by tracing the item through the instruction and thence to the objectives.

From this discussion it should have become clear that the abstract structure of instruction is in reality a rigorously explicit statement of how instructional programs are derived. And it should be equally clear that, in the absence of such a theory, it is impossible to develop anything but the most nebulous theory of achievement testing and evaluation. No pretense is made that an adequate theory is presently in existence. The areas of both curriculum and evaluation have remained almost wholly innocent of any attempt to provide an explicit or even a rational basis for its practice. Rather, the point of this discussion was to show why such a theory must be developed.

Assigning a Structure to the Question

The third type of activity involved in item-writing research consists in assigning a structure to the item. The chief problem here is how to state the structure of the item at the same level of abstraction as the segment of the instruction to which the item corresponds. This is best seen from an example. Figure 22 shows one of the several strategies

---

Statement of topic-sentence questions:
  a. Where do animals build their nests?
  b. Why do animals build their nests in inaccessible places?
  c. How do animals protect their young?
Location of the text essential for answering the questions:
  d. Birds build their nests in trees in order to protect their young from ground animals.
  e. Rabbits dig burrows under the ground for the purpose of protecting baby rabbits from owls, hawks, and large ground animals.
  f. Turtles dig holes and bury their eggs in the sand to prevent birds and man from finding and eating them.
Comparison of terms in the sentence to terms in the text:
  g. birds, rabbits, turtles → animals
  h. build, dig, build → build
  i. their nests, burrows, holes → nests
Derivation of the underlying sentence:
  j. Animals build their nests in inaccessible places for the purpose of protecting their young.
  etc.

Fig. 22. Partial definition of a topic-sentence question

NOTE: This illustration should not be interpreted as representing an acceptable definition. Some details remain unspecified and the definition in its present form applies only to a portion of the other questions which seem to be of the same type.

by which *topic sentence* questions of the type shown in lines (*a*), (*b*), and (*c*) might be defined. The strategy begins by deriving the sentence, line (*j*), underlying the questions. This is done from both an inspection of the text and an inspection of the questions. The convention of deriving this sentence is not strictly necessary. But it does seem to aid in both the development and the statement of the item definitions. In linguistics we would omit the underlying sentence out of parsimony, but in item-writing theory this kind of parsimony criterion should be regarded as an aesthetic value only.

A critical step is determining precisely the segment of the text to which the questions are relevant. In this case the relevant sentences are those shown in lines (*d*), (*e*), and (*f*). These sentences may be widely separated by intervening sentences or they may be contiguous. When they are separated, the intervening material must be deleted from the analysis, but eventually rules must be stated to describe the deletion process. Notice that sentences (*d*), (*e*), and (*f*) are all stated in a form such that their structures are parallel. This was not the case in the original text in which they were found. Their structures were transformed, with their paraphrase equivalence to the original preserved, as an aid in looking for regularities in their relationship to the underlying sentence.

The final step consists in looking for the relationships between the elements in the underlying sentence and the elements in the text. In this case the elements in the underlying sentence turned out to be including synonyms of the elements having parallel functions in the text sentences. Thus, the underlying sentence, and hence the questions, had to be stated at a level of abstraction sufficient to include the entire section of text to which it was relevant.

The derivation shown in figure 22 may not be considered adequate to define the item type. It can generate only an extremely limited range of the items which we ordinarily class as topic-sentence items and which bear obvious structural similarities to the one actually defined. For example, this derivation could not have been applied if the phrase *to prevent birds and man from finding and eating them* had not appeared in sentence (*j*). Also, the definition provides no way to distinguish between items made from contiguous, and items made from separated, sentences.

DEVISING RULES TO RELATE ITEMS TO THE INSTRUCTION

The rules for relating items to the instruction must meet at least five criteria. First, the items that result from the application of a rule must be intuitively meaningful. It is an easy matter to invent definitions of items which test behaviors no one really wants to test, say items to test students' verbatim memory of the sentences in instruction. There are many items testing behaviors to which we attach considerable value, and it is to the definition of those items that research energy should be directed. This injunction should not, however, interfere with the development of a good research strategy, and this strategy seems to dictate that the simpler items should be defined first.

Second, the rules should permit item writers working completely independently to replicate each other's work. To meet this criterion the rules must be completely explicit and must not require the item writer to employ subjective judgments. For example, the semantic-substitution procedure might at first glance appear to require the item writer to introspect about the meanings of words. This is not the case. The synonymity of terms can almost always be objectively determined from the instruction itself and can always be determined from the abstract structure of the instruction. Even in content areas which are poorly structured, it is possible to obtain replicable results by an empirical method such as giving groups of experts in those areas appropriately designed association tasks.

Third, redundancy should be avoided. There is little point in having two rules which produce exactly the same set of items. The more convenient rule should be retained and the other discarded. However, before one rule is discarded, care should be taken to show that the rules are indeed identical.

Fourth, new descriptive devices such as semantic-substitute procedures and the like should not be introduced if an existing device is capable of generating the same items. This criterion is essential if some degree of coherence and order in the development of rules is to be preserved. It also simplifies the task of the item writer.

Fifth, a rule should be as exhaustive, or as general, as possible. It should generate all the items which seem to the intuition of the investigator to measure the same thing and to bear some structural similarity. Minor rules can always be devised to further divide item populations into subsets whenever that appears to be desirable. Rules which do not meet this criteron may be of interest to researchers, but they should not be proposed for use in practical situations.

Objectives and Methods of Research on Achievement Test Items

5

The purpose of this volume is to help provide the basis for the scientific study of achievement test items. We began by developing descriptions of achievement test items which are sufficiently operationally replicable to meet the requirements for developing a science of achievement testing. Every science must be based upon a descriptive system which makes it possible to give rigorous definitions of the phenomena it studies. Owing to the absence of such a descriptive system in achievement testing there has been no way to interpret and accurately communicate the results of empirical research in the area. As a result, whatever knowledge has been gained in the area of achievement testing has remained largely pragmatic and largely a property of the inner intuitive processes of a few practicing artists. Now that we have developed a method of deriving item definitions which are sufficiently operational to fulfill the basic descriptive requirements of science, we should turn our attention to some of the other problems involved in developing a science of achievement testing.

There seem to be three logical divisions in achievement test theory: (*a*) the development of descriptive systems for defining items, which we will call *item-writing theory;* (*b*) the study of the processes underlying the responses to items, which we will refer to as *item-response theory;* and (*c*) the study of the relationship of responses on test items to responses to the real-world situations referred to by the instruction and presumably indexed by the responses to the achievement test items. This will be labeled *item-validity theory.*

What follows is a discussion of the objectives of the research in these three areas and a few comments on the research methods used.

ITEM-WRITING THEORY

The objective of item-writing theory is not just to systematically define and catalogue item types already in use, although this is certainly an important and creative part of the work in this area. Rather the skill of being able to define items must be regarded as part of the research skills which should be taught in the repertoire of any investigator performing educational research. Consequently, the basic research responsibility in item-writing theory consists in developing the descriptive devices used to define items.

The research directed at developing descriptive devices can be analyzed into two types of study—that directed at explicating the structure underlying instruction and that directed at developing new derivational algorithms such as the wh- transformation and the semantic-substitution rules. The object of explicating the structure of instruction is always to obtain a basis for defining item types. To illustrate, suppose we wished to define items testing knowledge of concepts taught in the instruction such as *Give two examples of an x, What are x and y examples of?* or *Mark the pictures* (of objects not included in the instruction) *which are x's.* The first step will be to state rules for identifying in a reproducible and verifiable manner the rule and example statements in instruction. To differentiate between items testing discovery and rote learning of concepts, order rules will have to be stated.

The research directed at developing new algorithms for deriving items follows much the same pattern. The object of this work is always to obtain the basis for defining items. For example, to define transfer items we will have to devise algorithms for deducting statements from the instruction. Propositional logic contains a number of algorithms which can probably be adapted to serve this purpose. But a considerable amount of analysis will have to be done before these algorithms can be applied in a replicable and verifiable manner.

When an investigator proposes a new algorithm, he must be able to demonstrate either that it is superior to an algorithm already in use at performing the same task or that it can be used to define items not definable by the presently used devices. Superiority would be demonstrated if the new device were shown to be easier to use or could define items not definable using existing algorithms in current use. It should go without saying that any algorithm should involve only objective procedures.

It is almost inevitable that the research in item-writing theory will produce new types of items which appear to be psychologically meaningful. And of course these events should not be ignored, but the invention of new item types is a secondary function of item-writing theory. Item-writing theory should probably be regarded as primarily a basic research methodology, rather than as an empirical science. The invention of new types of items, on the other hand, depends heavily upon theory in substantive areas such as cognitive psychology.

ITEM-RESPONSE THEORY

Item-response theory should be clearly distinguished from item-writing theory. Item-writing theory sets out to define item populations for the purposes of demonstrating the logical relevance of items to instruction and of providing operationally meaningful referents for the basic concepts used in testing, the classes of test items. On the other hand, item-response theory sets out to identify and describe the cognitive processes by which the student derives the correct answers to a class of items and to determine how to employ items in observing those processes of interest.

Those holding to the traditional views of the nature of achievement test items have often claimed that it is useless to study the processes underlying the responses to a class of items. They contend that it would be easy to change the processes underlying the responses simply by changing the instruction to which the items are relevant. For example, they would argue that it is useless to study the processes underlying the question *What color is the house?* which is relevant to the instruction *The house is green,* because whatever one found certainly would not apply if one changed the instruction to *The house blended with the foliage.* And indeed, for as long as we accepted the notion that it was somehow possible to meaningfully define a class of items independent of the instruction to which the items are relevant, this argument presented us with insurmountable problems which caused scientists to abandon any hope of studying the processes underlying item responses. This has left the field to those who ply the quasi-mystical crafts of the present-day achievement test writer.

But the claim can now be seen to be fallacious, for it rests upon the assumption that we can somehow change the structure of the instruction without simultaneously changing the classes into which we would place the items originally derived from that instruction. Specifically, those people would seem to believe that, just because the question in the example just cited retains the same physical form, this item must therefore remain exactly the same type of item regardless of how the instruction to which it is relevant is changed. Since we now see *that an item's type is determined by the relationship of that item to the structure of the instruction to which it is relevant,* we can reject not only this fallacy but the argument it seems to support.

Now, suppose we did perform extensive studies to determine what processes underlie a particular class of items. Also, suppose that, after doing so, we retained those items in exactly the same physical form but changed the structure of the instruction to which these items were relevant. Subsequent studies would undoubtedly show that this operation had indeed changed the nature of the processes underlying the responses. But this would in no way damage the scientific usefulness of the results of either set of studies. By changing the structure of the instruction to which our items were relevant we simultaneously changed the classifications to which the items belonged, and we were no longer studying the same class of items. Therefore, the results of our second set of studies would be relevant to quite a different class of items. The fact that the physical forms of the items happened to be the same in the two sets of studies is regarded as perhaps misleading to a few, but it is definitely irrelevant when adequate definitions of item classes are used.

In the past there was little to be gained from performing experiments which attempted to analyze the cognitive processes underlying responses to a class of items. It was, of course, generally recognized that the process underlying the responses to one class of items undoubtedly differed in important ways from the processes underlying the responses to other classes of items. Indeed, it was because of this realization that major efforts (Bloom 1956) were made to taxonomize different item types. But, in the absence of operational methods of defining classes of items, there was no way to say what the results of an experiment meant, because there was no way to identify the populations of items to which the results were attributable or to distinguish those populations to which the results were not attributable. As a result, identifying the processes underlying the responses to a class of items has been based almost wholly upon loose psychologizing and introspection.

One objective of item-response theory may be said to be to develop the knowledge which will permit us to design tests having exactly the properties we choose and to do so entirely from a priori considerations. When item research was carried on in the past, it consisted in starting with the collection of items which constituted a particular test and then studying the properties of just those items. But such studies were of little value for developing a theoretical science of achievement testing. In the absence of item definitions, there was no way to identify what kind of items were being studied, and consequently there was no way to say whether the results would generalize to other items not included in the test. Ad hoc studies of this sort may have some temporal value, but they contribute little to our basic understanding of achievement testing.

Item-response studies have two specific objectives. The first is to analyze and describe the processes underlying the responses to the different classes of items. The second is to determine how to employ items in order to observe some processes of particular interest. But before discussing either type of research it seems to be necessary first to discuss some basic issues in the design of research on item-response theory; for, with the exception of the study of Hively et al. (1968), it appears that psychologists have failed to grasp the basic criteria a research design must meet if it is to accomplish anything of real scientific value.

Studies in item-response research must meet three criteria of special interest. First, the investigator must offer objective definitions of the classes of items he is studying. Item-response studies are designed to discover the properties of item populations. In the absence of objective definitions of those populations, no one can be certain what classes of items are being studied or to what class of items the results should be attributed.

Second, the investigator must follow some procedure (preferably a random selection procedure) for assuring that the sample of items he draws is not a biased sample of the class of items being studied. In the absence of such a procedure, the experimenter cannot reject the assertion that the results are attributable to some sort of bias in the way in which he selected items. Specifically, the results of an item-response study must be generalizable to a population of items if the results are to be of any scientific merit. And no such generalization is possible when a bias could have been introduced by the manner in which the items were selected.

Finally, in performing statistical tests of the significance of the results of an experiment the investigator must employ designs appropriate for dual sampling studies. In item-response studies, observed differences can arise as a result of chance factors either in drawing the sample of subjects or in drawing the sample of items. Consequently, differences observed in item-response studies must be tested using error terms which include estimates of the sampling error arising from *both* sources.

Consider a study by Karraker (1967) which seems fairly typical of the item-response research currently being reported. He set out to determine if the plausible wrong responses occurring in multiple-choice tests were remembered as being the correct responses by both students who were and students who were not given knowledge of results after they had taken a test. He began by giving the students a forty-item multiple-choice test. Then in a subsequent session the tests were returned to one group, and the items along with the correct responses read to the students in the group, while another group received no knowledge of results. Both of these groups, along with a third which had not taken the test, were then given a test containing the same question stems but on which they had to construct the responses. The experimenter then scored the number of wrong alternatives from the multiple-choice test that occurred as responses in the constructed-response test. From his discussion of the results it was clear that the investigator was claiming that his results were generalizable to all items in all achievement tests.

Obviously, no such generalization was justified. To begin with, the investigator failed to establish the basis for his claim that his items were actually achievement test items. While he did say that the items covered various topics in educational psychology and that the students were enrolled in a course having that title, he did not mention taking any precaution to assure that the items tested instruction actually presented to the students. So it was by no means certain that the items were even achievement test items and not some sort of general-knowledge or aptitude items. Therefore, we cannot be sure whether his results are actually attributable to achievement test items.

Second, it hardly requires pointing out that the items were probably not representative of *all* achievement test items, even though the investigator claimed that his results held for all achievement test items. The investigator did not claim that he had used any sampling scheme whatever in collecting the items for his test. This should not be regarded as a trivial matter, for it seems unlikely that the effect he was investigating will hold for all types of test items. For example, arithmetic computation items may be solved de novo with each test administration. This reduces the likelihood of a remembered wrong response occurring on a second test. The same may be true of any type of item for which the student places no particular value on remembering the answer, because the instruction has been designed to teach general problem-solving algorithms rather than particular responses. Therefore, this study, like many other studies in item-response research, is subject to the criticism that the items were drawn in a biased manner.

Third, suppose the investigator had acceptably defined his items and sampled randomly from the population of items defined. He still could not have generalized his results to the items in that population, because he did not apply the proper statistical analysis to his data. He employed a two-factor analysis of variance design having the three treatments in one factor and two levels of ability in the other factor. His error term was based only on the variance between students.

This design totally ignored the facts that he included only a sample of items in his study and that his results could have occurred just because he was studying a biased sample. He should have used something like a three by two by forty (items) design with repeated measures on the factor for items. By treating the items as a random factor, he could estimate the amount of error variance associated with drawing a sample from the item population he was studying. And by adding this error term to the error term calculated from the between-student variance, he could obtain an error term which would estimate the error associated with simultaneously drawing samples of students and items. Only by comparing his observed difference with this combined error term would he be justified in claiming that his observed difference had some particular probability of occurring.

However, even if he had applied the correct statistical techniques, the investigator still would not have been justified in claiming that his results were generalizable to items derived from other instructional programs. Since he presumably drew his items just from those applying to a single program, that program is the only one to which he can rationally generalize his results.

It may seem a bit harsh to criticize this study, since the investigator did not have access to item definitions, but this would completely miss the point. These criticisms have said nothing that is not printed in the standard textbooks on research design. Yet, the study is quite representative[1] of the studies currently being published. It is to be hoped that in the future investigators will employ designs of the level of sophistication exemplified by Hively et al. (1968).

The processes underlying responses to a class of items can be studied through at least two major approaches. The first consists in identifying all the different processes or strategies students use to derive correct responses to a class of items and the conditions under which each strategy can and cannot be used. The second approach is to study the hierarchical relationships among the processes underlying responses to different classes of items. The object of this research is, of course, to determine how to employ test items in such a manner that we can unambiguously observe the processes in which we are interested.

There are no studies, known to the author, which have attempted to analyze the strategies students use to derive correct answers to a class of items. The custom has been to accept the test author's claims about what underlying processes were tested by an item. And, since there were no operational methods for defining classes of items, it was not scientifically very useful to present empirical challenges to the test author's claims. Item-response research can be commenced now that it is possible to give a clear definition of the items being studied, and we can feel confident that the discussions will not degenerate into disputes about

1. It was selected by picking the first report on item-response research from the journal on top of a rather messy stack lying beside my chair. Upon further examination of the same issue, it was seen that other studies could have provided equally useful examples for this discussion.

whether two different investigators are talking about the same or different classes of items.

One might say that item-response research is based on the propositions that (*a*) there are probably several strategies students can use to answer a class of items and (*b*) the conditions of testing and instruction determine which of those strategies are possible in a given situation.

To illustrate,[2] consider the rote, wh- question *Who hit the ball?* which was derived from the sentence *The boy hit the ball.* This type of item is commonly used in achievement tests because it seems to be popularly believed by test makers that it tests students' knowledge of the content presented in the instruction. This assumption may be true in some testing situations, but its truth is doubtful in others. Even very young children, four and five years old, can correctly answer questions like *Who wugged the durf?* after they have been read the sentence *The bofud wugged the durf.* Since this sentence contains nonsense morphemes in place of lexical morphemes, the sentence cannot be said to contain knowledge in the usual sense of that word. Therefore, we might conclude that some process in addition to the one popularly assumed must underlie the responses to questions of this type.

It seems to be convenient for some to state theories about the nature of the processes underlying responses in the form of instructions to a computer which is programmed to simulate the same behaviors. What seems to be the simplest progam which would simulate the behaviors just described would include instructions which would perform these operations: (*a*) Read in the sentence and store it. (*b*) Read in the question and store it. (*c*) Compare each word in the question to each word in the sentence, deleting those words for which matches are obtained. (*d*) Print out the words remaining in the sentence. The printout represents the correct answer.

The chief advantage of expressing theories in this form is that doing so permits us to state alternative theories with sufficient precision to distinguish them from each other. For example, children of nine and ten years of age answer many questions correctly when, instead of the sentence, they are given only the lexical words from the sentence

2. Because of the newness of item-response research it seems advisable to cite studies illustrating approaches to item-response problems. Since there is a scarcity of such research I have elected to describe some pilot studies I am conducting at the University of Chicago and to mention one I conducted in cooperation with Dr. Milagros Aquino while she was at the Southwest Regional Laboratory in Los Angeles. She is now a faculty member at Los Angeles State College. All the studies were designed for purely exploratory purposes and should be regarded merely as illustrations rather than as formal research reports. The reader is cautioned against placing much faith in the results described.

arranged in a random order. Correct answers occur when either natural-language or nonsense words are used in this way. To instruct a computer to do the same, we would have to expand the program described above to include a device to store in the computer a list and a small set of rules that permit the machine to add the appropriate structure words to the answer.

It should be added, however, that when sentences are replaced by randomly ordered word lists, we have not yet found a reasonably general or economical way to program a machine to answer questions in which two or more words were deleted. Also, we have observed that students occasionally give the correct answers to the questions made from natural-language sentences when presented with no sentence of any form. We know of no way to represent this process in a reasonably general form, either.

It is possible, and even easier, to express these theories using transformations, semantic substitutions, and other descriptive devices like those used in item-writing theory. The only objection which might be raised against this practice is that, unless the theory is clearly labeled for what it is, it may be readily confused with item definitions. And, of course, item definitions in no way purport to describe the manner in which a student derives his response to questions.

The particular process a student uses to derive his response may depend upon conditions in the instruction and testing. In the pilot studies, children seemed to give many correct responses to the sentences containing the nonsense words when each question was presented immediately following the presentation of the sentence, and fewer correct responses when a ten-second counting task was interpolated. None were observed when a full day was allowed to elapse. Correct answers to meaningful sentences seemed to show some decrease over time, also, but the amount of the decrease was much less. While these data were collected in a manner that did not permit the interaction to be tested for significance, the effects were strong enough to make the same outcome seem somewhat likely when the formal studies are conducted. If we can assume that, when an item is actually testing knowledge of the content, retention will be greater than when the question is testing other types of processes, and if we can imagine that an interaction actually occurs, then we can interpret these results as showing that wh-rote items are less likely to test knowledge of the content of instruction when they are given immediately following instruction than when some delay is interpolated between the question and the response.

All the results mentioned so far were obtained by presenting one sentence-question pair at a time. To determine if the instructional setting influenced the response data, the sentences were also presented in the context of the paragraphs from which they were drawn. In the nonsense versions, all lexical morphemes were replaced with pronounceable nonsense syllables, and the inflectional and derivational morphemes were retained along with the structure words. The question immediately followed the presentation of the paragraph. There were few correct responses to the nonsense versions, and both versions seemed to be more difficult under this condition than when the sentences were presented in isolation. But, again, the groups used in the two experiments were not strictly comparable. If the scores for the embedded sentences were really lower, then this result might be interpreted as indicating that the questions given under this condition were more likely to be testing knowledge of the content than when the same questions were presented for isolated sentences. The effects of forgetting could have also explained this set of results, of course.

These pilot studies are presented merely to illustrate the general approach to item-response questions, not to convince anyone of the truth of the results. But the specific features of the design may be of some interest. The paragraphs were randomly drawn from textbooks which were randomly selected from a fairly comprehensive list of hardbound texts used in grades four through six. The sentences were randomly drawn from each paragraph, and the node tested in each sentence was randomly selected. The designs involved randomly assigning subjects to questions, and questions were completely confounded with students, so that generalizations about both students and questions were justified.

But the deficiencies should also be noted. As already mentioned, the numbers of students were small and the groups were often not comparable. Further, the .10 level of confidence was the criterion for rejecting the null hypothesis. More important, control data should have been consistently obtained from students given just the question without the instruction, and possibly from students given a task which seemed fairly likely to actually test knowledge of the content of the sentences stated in natural language.

The objective of the second type of item-response research is to determine how test items should be employed so that those processes in which we are particularly interested can be observed. Gagné (1967), in the paper mentioned above, has pointed out that test results are always ambiguous unless we take into account the hierarchical relationships among the capabilities being tested. Because this notion is of fundamental importance in achievement testing, it will be explored in some detail here. We shall begin by presenting the basic concept of hierarchies of response capabilities, then examine some of its consequences for test design, and finally discuss deductions which can be made from the hierarchical model and how these deductions can be subjected to experimental tests in order to analyze the hierarchies underlying the responses to test items.

Much of the behavior we teach in instruction is conceptualized as being hierarchical. For example, if we wish to teach students the capability of solving multiplication problems, we usually effect this objective by teaching a number of capabilities in a definite sequence. This sequence may begin with instruction in counting and simple addition and terminate with instruction in multiplication. Each capability taught in such a sequence is thought to be an essential component of a more complex capability subsequently taught. An entire set of capabilities related in this way is called a hierarchy.

These hierarchies may be represented by diagrams such as the one in figure 23. This diagram shows that the correct performance of

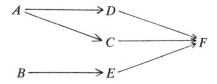

Fig. 23. Diagram of a hierarchy of behavior capabilities

capability F depends upon the correct performance of capabilities D, C, and E; that both capabilities D and C depend upon capability A; and so on.

Responses which are thought to index these capabilities are observed using test items. These items and their responses may be incorporated into diagrams of the sort shown in Figure 24. This diagram shows just the chain A-D-F. The item thought to test a given capability, say D, is represented by T_D, and the response thought to index that capability is represented by R_D.

Gagné's argument began with the assertion that, if we observe a correct response to an item, say T_F, we may interpret that response in either of two ways. The student may have actually acquired capability F, or the student may not have acquired capability F but was able to answer the item correctly using some other capability. For example, he

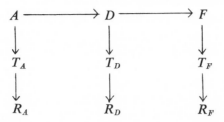

Fig. 24. Diagram of the operationalization of a hierarchy of capabilities

can obtain the answer to multiplication problems by multiplying, by repeated additions, by copying from another test paper, and so on. Should the student respond incorrectly to T_F, this response could also be interpreted in at least two ways. Either the student failed to learn capability F or he failed to acquire some simpler capability, some capability to its left.

There are compelling reasons for eliminating these ambiguities in the interpretation of test items. The most important use of achievement test results is to determine what a student has failed to learn and what a program has failed to teach. Instructional decisions must be based upon this type of information. All other uses are of secondary importance. It should be clear that no matter how much we know about the processes underlying the responses to a class of items, these ambiguities must still be contended with.

For the purpose of reducing these ambiguities, Gagné suggested that we use two-stage testing designs. For example, if a student fails to demonstrate capability F and also fails to demonstrate capability D when D, C, and E are tested, then we would not attribute his failure to a failure to learn F but rather to a failure to learn capability D, which is prerequisite to a correct performance of capability F.

On the other hand, correct responses to test items are inherently ambiguous, for it can never be shown conclusively that the student has indeed learned the capability the item is designed to test. This should be viewed as an instance of the familiar problem that, while it is always possible to prove that a false statement is false, it is never possible to prove that a true statement is true. Suppose the student gave correct responses to all the items testing capabilities A through F. This would certainly strengthen our confidence that a correct response to the item of interest to us, T_F, demonstrated that the student had really learned capability F. But it would only demonstrate that the student *could* have learned F. There would remain a possibility that the student had obtained his answer using some process other than F.

Other items could be devised to test and possibly eliminate each of the irrelevant processes by which the student could have obtained the correct response. But a correct response on any one of those items would be subject to the same ambiguities, and it would be necessary to use still other items to eliminate them. This fact should demonstrate that we would be forced into an almost infinite sequence of testing without really resolving the ambiguity. But, even if nothing but negative responses were observed to the items used in an attempt to reduce the ambiguity of the response to the item which is actually of interest to us, we would still be unable to refute the argument that the student may have answered the item of interest using some process we know nothing about.

This argument definitely does not show that two-stage measurement designs are useless. What it does show is that the interpretation of tests depends upon our empirical knowledge of the processes underlying responses and that we can use the knowledge we gain from item-response studies to reduce the major sources of ambiguity in interpreting test results. Some ambiguity can be reduced by manipulating the conditions of instruction and testing, and a very substantial amount of the remaining ambiguity can be eliminated by two-stage testing designs which take into account the hierarchical relationships among the processes being tested.

To analyze the hierarchical relationships among the processes underlying the responses to items, we will require the use of designs somewhat different from those generally in use in educational research. An analysis of the properties ascribed to hierarchies suggests several useful approaches. What follows is a brief discussion of some of the possible approaches. Specifically, it is meant to be only an illustration of the inferential structures that are possible; it is not offered as an exhaustive investigation of the consequences which follow from the hierarchy model.

The simplest analysis arises as a consequence of the assertion that a student cannot perform a task requiring a complex capability until he has learned the simpler component capabilities. Hence, a student cannot perform capability F until he has learned capability D, if D is actually a component of F. Suppose we start with a sample consisting of students who have learned neither D nor F and split them into two groups. If we give one group training designed to teach just the capability F, it would not be unreasonable to expect a number of students to *discover* the capabilities involved in D. So the training would result in an increase on both T_F and T_D for that group. But if the other group were given training designed to teach just D we would expect members of that group to show an increase on T_D while their responses to T_F remain unchanged. Casting these results into a two treatments by two tests analysis of variance design would show a significant treatment by test interaction, if D were in fact a component of F.

Hively et al. (1968) have pointed out another consequence deductible from the hierarchy model. Suppose we have six populations of items, one population for testing each of the capabilities diagrammed in figure 23. We would expect the items within a single population to be relatively homogeneous with respect to difficulty, in view of the fact that all measure the same underlying capability. But we would expect the items in different populations to differ considerably in difficulty because the underlying processes differ in complexity. Hively performed this type of study using items drawn from the populations generated with his universe definitions of arithmetic problems. His analysis of variance showed exactly this pattern.

This analysis can be formalized and carried a bit further in making predictions. The responses to the test items, say to T_D, depend upon two conditions—first that the student has acquired the capabilities unique to D, which we will represent as d, and second that the student has acquired the capability unique to the components of A, which in this case would be a. Hence, we can represent the probability of a correct response in item population T_D as

$$p(D) = p_a \times p_d,$$

provided we can assume that the probabilities of learning the unique components a and d are independent. This assumption is not intuitively unreasonable,[3] since we commonly observe situations in which students can correctly perform all the operations uniquely involved in multiplication but are unable to correctly perform some of the addition operations in multiplication problems.

Continuing this reasoning, we can derive the functions shown in table 1. Under any reasonable assumptions about the magnitudes of the probabilities associated with the unique components, it should be possible to obtain a rough prediction of the rank order of the mean difficulties of the items in the item samples being studied. This is illus-

3. In those cases where it does not seem reasonable to assume independence of learning a and b, it is necessary to resort to the use of Markovian probability models for these analyses.

TABLE 1

Functions expressing the probabilities associated with a correct response on tests measuring capabilities shown in figure 23

Functions	Mean Item Difficulties Assuming that $p_x = .5$ in All Cases
$p(A) = p_a$	.5000
$p(B) = p_b$	.5000
$p(D) = p_a \times p_d$	.2500
$p(C) = p_a \times p_c$	.2500
$p(E) = p_b \times p_e$	.2500
$p(F) = p_a \times p_b \times p_d \times p_c \times p_e \times p_f$	.0156

trated in table 1 where it was assumed that all probabilities are .5. A similar argument based on the binomial theorem would show that the variances among difficulties of items in the item samples should increase directly with the complexity of the underlying capabilities the samples of items measure.

Following much the same form of reasoning, we should be able to predict roughly the relative sizes of the intercorrelations among the scores obtained from tests measuring capabilities which are hierarchically related. The variation in scores on a test, say T_D, may be attributed to three sources of variability—variations in the students' capabilities unique to A, variations in the students' capabilities unique to D, and error of observation. This can be expressed formally as

$$s_D^2 = s_a^2 + s_d^2 + s_\epsilon^2,$$

where s_D^2 is variability on T_D and s_x^2 is variability in the component unique to capability X. Table 2 shows a breakdown of the variance

TABLE 2

Analysis of the variance components of tests measuring the capabilities represented in the hierarchy shown in figure 23

$$s_A^2 = s_a^2 + s_\epsilon^2$$
$$s_B^2 = s_b^2 + s_\epsilon^2$$
$$s_D^2 = s_a^2 + s_d^2 + s_\epsilon^2$$
$$s_C^2 = s_a^2 + s_c^2 + s_\epsilon^2$$
$$s_E^2 = s_b^2 + s_e^2 + s_\epsilon^2$$
$$s_F^2 = s_a^2 + s_b^2 + s_d^2 + s_c^2 + s_e^2 + s_f^2 + s_\epsilon^2$$

components of tests measuring each of the capabilities represented by the hierarchy shown in figure 23.

Notice that s_A^2 and s_D^2 share one component in common. There are similar overlaps in many of the other test variances shown. If we assume that all variances attributable to unique capabilities, s_x^2, are approximately equal, we can say (ignoring s_ϵ^2) that roughly one-half of the total variance in the two tests is shared variation. Table 3 shows

TABLE 3

Predicted percentages of shared variation among tests
measuring the capabilities represented in figure 23

Tests	A	B	D	C	E	F
A	—					
B	.00	—				
D	.50	.00	—			
C	.50	.00	.33	—		
E	.00	.50	.00	.00	—	
F	.17	.17	.33	.33	.33	—

the percentage of variance shared by each of the pairs of tests measuring the capabilities represented in figure 23. The error variances are assumed to be uncorrelated, and therefore they do not need to be considered in calculating the shared variation. Presumably, the intercorrelations among the tests would be roughly proportional to the square roots of the numbers shown in this table. Path analyses could then be used to test the hypotheses represented by such a table.

Up to this point no mention has been made of the fact that it is possible to analyze the processes specific to answering the item, itself. These processes can be analyzed separately from the capability underlying the responses to an item, since it is possible to test the same underlying capability using two or more items. For example, Hively et al. (1968) show items like

$$\frac{17}{\times 5} \quad \text{and} \quad 17 \times 5 = \underline{\qquad}$$

as alternative forms for testing the same underlying capability. By noting the differences in difficulties of the two test forms we can investigate the process specific to a particular form of an item.

It is difficult to overemphasize the importance to instruction of research which attempts to analyze the cognitive processes underlying responses to item types. It is commonly accepted that, in many subject-matter areas, the learning of the knowledge explicitly taught by the instructional programs is less valued as a learning outcome than learning the complex cognitive processes by which that and other knowledge is discovered, evaluated, organized, and applied. Achievement test items which can test these complex processes are useful not only for evaluating the student's achievement and the effectiveness of his in-

81

struction but also for providing the instructional exercises which force him to practice those processes. But few of these benefits can be reaped until we can identify exactly what it is that the different classes of items test.

ITEM-VALIDITY THEORY

The objective of item-validity research is to study the relationship of responses on test items to responses in the real-world situations referred to by the instruction. Instruction seldom has as its objective the teaching of the ability to respond correctly just to a test item. Rather, the ultimate goals of instruction are usually to influence behaviors which the student will employ outside the controlled environment in which instruction and achievement testing occur. For example, instruction in driver training may have as one of its ultimate goals teaching the students to observe appropriate behaviors under adverse driving conditions. Yet the achievement test given may be a pencil and paper test of the students' knowledge of the statements made during instruction rather than an observation of their performances under conditions referred to by the instruction. Responses to test items are presently merely assumed to index in some way the behaviors students exhibit under the conditions referred to by the instruction. The object of item-validity research is to systematically test this assumption.

There was little point in testing these assumptions as long as the results could be generalized to just the items on a single test. By the time the results were known, the instruction was likely to have changed and a new test would be in use. But when the results of studies can be generalized to a whole class of items which are derivable from a broad range of instructional programs, the study of item validity assumes considerably greater theoretical and practical significance.

But before the urge to rush out to do item-validity research becomes overwhelming, it should be pointed out that several important developments must take place before it is possible to do scientifically viable work in this area. To mention the most important, there is no way to demonstrate logically the relevance of most instruction to any event in the real world. Most instruction takes place by the transmittal of information which is encoded in some system of symbols. That is, the symbols refer to objects, events, and so on, which are not the symbols themselves.

If we should set out to demonstrate the logical relevance of instruction to events in the real world, we would have to devise a set of rules for deriving the symbols used in instruction from the objects, events, and so on, in the real world. Our problem arises from the fact that no one knows how to do this in a manner sufficiently rigorous to make the results objectively replicable. It is true that semanticists have been studying this problem for some time, but so far logicians and the semanticists' fellow linguists remain singularly unimpressed by the results. Pending major advances in the study of semantics, we will probably have to continue our present practice of doing either bad research in item validity or, as is more usually the case in this area, no research at all.

The chief reason for introducing the item-validity research here was to draw an important distinction that might otherwise cause confusions in item-writing and item-response theory. Neither of these branches of achievement test theory either can or should attempt to show the relevance of instruction to any event outside the instructional situation. To attempt to do so would only muddle the discourse in those areas. And what may be worse, muddling the discussion would only divert attention and energy away from the socially and scientifically important work to be accomplished in the theories of item response and item writing.

A FINAL REMARK

It should not be thought that the concepts of item response and item validity originate here. Both have been discussed by numerous authors. However, because there was no way to define populations of achievement test items apart from a specific test, the earlier discussions have been received by researchers as statements of the inner hopes of those authors but not regarded as worth the efforts or serious consideration of theory-oriented scientists. It is hoped that this work has provided the necessary theoretical framework within which research in the theories of item writing and item response can be carried on in a scientifically useful manner.

Appendix

by Peter Menzel

The Linguistic Bases of the Theory of Writing Items for Instruction Stated in Natural Language

INTRODUCTORY REMARKS

A grammar is an attempt to make explicit the linguistic knowledge the native speaker/hearer[1] has about his language. The job of making explicit our intuitive knowledge of our native language is accomplished with more or less success by different grammarians depending not only on their own knowledge, sophistication, ability to communicate, etc.; but, equally important, depending on their "philosophy of language." That is, just as it is impossible for the most knowledgeable and sophisticated physicist to give a systematic description (one that integrates all the known facts) of the universe in terms of a model which is based on a flat earth, so it is impossible for the most knowledgeable and sophisticated linguist to give a sytematic description of any language in terms of a model which oversimplifies the structure of language, or confuses syntax with semantics, etc.

Although this is not the place to justify any particular philosophy

The sections entitled "Transformational Analysis," "Anaphora Analysis," and "Intersentence Syntax" were originally developed for Bormuth's Readability Project. These analyses were in some degree further refined and extended, and the "Part of Speech" and "Sentence Type" analyses developed with the support of the Southwest Regional Laboratory in Educational Research and Development. During the development of these papers I served as research assistant for the Air Force English Syntax Project at the University of California, Los Angeles. This experience along with the advice and instruction received from the principal investigators, R. P. Stockwell, P. Schachted, and B. H. Partee, contributed materially to the content of these papers.

1. In general, we do not need to differentiate between speaking and hearing (encoding and decoding) for our present purposes, and I will, therefore, use the terms *speaker* and *speaker/hearer* interchangeably. Where the need arises to draw the encoding-decoding dichotomy, I will use the two terms *speaker* and *hearer*.

of language, we need to discuss this question briefly because it is important in making explicit the application of the theory of testing discussed in the first part of this monograph. The theory of testing proposed there makes use of a particular theory of language, and if the reader is to use the testing procedures outlined there, he must be at least familiar with the theory of language underlying the testing theory.

The theory of language in question, which is based as is any other linguistic theory on the linguistic knowledge of the native speaker, is one that allows us to formalize certain relationships between linguistic structures (phrases, sentences, etc.) in a way which is particularly useful for the purpose of the theory of testing proposed. Needless to say, the theory of language was not conceived with this end in mind, but as a self-supporting system. Its usefulness to an explicit testing theory, therefore, constitutes what is called "independent support" for the theory of language. What is meant by this is simply the fact that any theory (or model) constructed for one set of circumstances (in this case the description of language) is said to receive independent support when it can predict the behavior of whatever it describes in an altogether different set of circumstances (in this case the testing theory proposed earlier).[2]

The theory of language underlying the following sections is, briefly, that of transformational-generative grammar. To justify the application of this theory to testing theory, it is necessary for me to show that transformational-generative grammar is able to systematically state the relationships between the linguistic structures (phrases, sentences, etc.) that are used in the theory of testing. This is actually a much simpler task than the justification of a theory of language per *explanation* of language. However, the two are very much interwoven, so that I will have to deal at least with some aspects of the explanation of language. Demonstrating the relationship between linguistic structures depends largely on proving that the *surface structure* (i.e., that structure of linguistic units which is immediately discernible) is not sufficient to describe syntactic processes and that, therefore, the linguist is forced to assume an *underlying* (or *deep*) *structure,* so-called because it underlies the surface structure.

The necessity for assuming deep structures can be shown by means of syntactic and semantic processes. Although these two aspects of

2. Note, incidentally, that "independent support" works both ways. That is, the theory of testing is supported by the fact that it can be formalized using an already existing system, namely, the grammar to be discussed below.

language are interrelated, I will attempt to discuss them separately below. The syntactic processes in question are three: structural ambiguities, related sentences, and apparent structural identities.

A sentence (phrase, etc.) is said to be structurally ambiguous when it has two or more meanings but only one surface structure and the ambiguity is not a semantic one. Semantic ambiguities are due to the fact that most words have more than one meaning; thus,

(1) Harry wore a light suit,

is semantically ambiguous between "a suit light in color" and "a suit light in weight." Structural ambiguity is not due to multiple meanings, but to the fact that the surface structure in question has two or more deep structures. This has been intuitively realized by a number of traditional grammarians, but it was transformational-generative grammar which first proposed a systematic way of handling this problem. Some well-known examples of structural ambiguity are

(2) i. Mary saw the boy walking to the railroad station.
    ii. The police stopped drinking at midnight.
    iii. John knows a taller man than Bill.

In (2i) either "Mary" or "the boy" could be doing the "walking"; in (2ii) either "the police" or "some unspecified offenders" could be doing the "drinking"; and in (2iii) "the man" can either be "taller than Bill is" or "taller than some other unspecified man whom Bill knows." To account for these ambiguities, the linguist assumes two different deep structures for each of the sentences in (2), where each deep structure represents one of the meanings of each sentence. The examples in (2) could be represented as having the following sentences underlying them:[3]

(3) i. Mary saw the boy.

$\begin{cases} a.\ \text{Mary was walking to the railroad station.} \\ b.\ \text{The boy was walking to the railroad station.} \end{cases}$

---

3. Deep structures are usually represented as "trees." To avoid introducing numerous difficult and for our purpose needless concepts into this already complex theoretical discussion, I will not use deep-structure trees; instead, I will use sentence-like representations which I hope will convey the intended structures. Needless to say, this practice is only a convenient shorthand and should not be confused with the use of deep structures as specified in linguistic theory.

ii. The police stopped.
$\left\{\begin{array}{l} a. \text{ The police drank at midnight.} \\ b. \text{ Someone drank at midnight.} \end{array}\right\}$

iii. John knows a man.
$\left\{\begin{array}{l} a. \text{ The man is taller than Bill is.} \\ b. \text{ The man is taller than a man} \\ \quad \text{(whom) Bill knows.} \end{array}\right\}$

As can be seen from the examples above, deep structures are more explicit than surface structures. That is, a deep structure contains all the information necessary for the syntactic and semantic interpretation of the surface structure in question.

There are two corollaries to this observation; the first is that a grammar that contains both a deep structure and a surface structure must also provide the user of the grammar with a way to get from the former to the latter. The second is that since surface structures can be ambiguous and are also otherwise "mutilated" with respect to their deep structures, the logical place in the grammar for the semantic component (i.e., that component which describes the meaning of the sentence) is also the deep structure.[4]

A way to map deep structures onto surface structures is provided by an operation, used in mathematics, called a *transformation*. In mathematics, transformations are operations which map strings of symbols onto other strings of symbols. For example, the ordered set of symbols consisting of all even numbers between two and ten (i.e., 2, 4, 6, 8, 10) can be mapped onto the ordered set of symbols consisting of all the odd numbers between nine and five (i.e., 9, 7, 5). In this example it is, of course, necessary to map more than one symbol of the original (input) string onto at least one symbol of the output string. In a similiar manner, it was necessary in the sentence of example (2) to map more than one symbol of the original string (the deep structure) onto the output string (the surface structure). The mathematical operations called transformations are thus parallel to the process needed in grammar even to the extent that they may lose information (be ambiguous) with respect to the input string. In addition, mathematical transformations can be specified in a systematic and unambiguous way. That is,

---

4. Notice that the second corollary places a very powerful constraint upon the deep structure, since this structure must be both syntactically and semantically explicit, in the sense that it must contain *all* the information necessary for both the semantic and the syntactic components of the grammar. Constraints of this nature, incidentally, are very important for a theory, because they act as built-in controls on the theory.

transformations can be stated in such a way that they can apply only to those strings the writer of the transformations wants them to apply, and in such a way that the change in the strings in question must occur in the manner the writer wants it to occur. Last, transformations can be stated so that they must fulfill Boolean conditions of analyzability; that is, the *structure* of the input string and its parts can be described, as well as the *structure* of the output string and its parts.

It seems clear that the operation discussed above is exactly the kind the grammarians want in order to describe the way to get from the deep structure of a sentence to its surface structure.[5]

Once introduced into linguistic theory, however, the transformational derivation of surface structures from deep structures is a powerful concept which should enable us to explain more than just structural ambiguities. And in fact, the linguistic theory sketched above accounts for both related sentences and apparent structural identities (which are really surface-structure identities), as well as providing the grammar with a place for the application of the semantic component without the need of some separate, unmotivated structure or level, because, as was already indicated, the semantic component can be applied to the deep structure which is needed in any case for a satisfactory account of the purely grammatical relationships.

Turning then to the related sentences, we can say that it has long been intuitively felt that sentences like the following are related:

(3)   i. John ate the meat.
     ii. Did John eat the meat?
     iii. Who ate the meat?
     iv. What did John eat?
     v. John didn't eat the meat.
     vi. Didn't John eat the meat?
     vii. The meat was eaten by John.

Using the notions sketched above of surface structures being transformationally derived from deep structures, the intuitively felt relationships between the sentences in example (4) can be described and

5. It is probably best to introduce another technical term here, namely, *derive*. Since surface structures are quite literally derived from deep structures, the former are also called *derived structures*. But, since it takes more than one transformation to get from a deep structure to a surface structure, all intermediate structures are also derived structures. Last, the deep structure(s), intermediate structures, and surface structure (of, e.g., a sentence) are called the *derivation* (of that sentence).

integrated into the whole system of the grammar. This is achieved in the following way: All the sentences in example (4) are assumed to have the same deep structure, except for minor differences that need not concern us here. The different surface structures are due to different transformations that were applied to the sentences in the course of their respective derivations.[6]

There are many sentences which have the same surface structure, but which behave differently with respect to the transformations that may be applied to them. A well-known example of a sentence pair of this type is

> (5) i. John expected the doctor to examine Bill.
> ii. John persuaded the doctor to examine Bill.

Judged from their surface structures, these two sentences appear to be identical. Notice, however, that these two sentences do not have the same pseudocleft form:

> (6) i. What John expected was for the doctor to examine Bill.
> ii. *What John persuaded was for the doctor to examine Bill.[7]

Nor does either of the two sentences have the same pseudocleft form of the following type:

> (7) i. *What John expected the doctor of was that he should examine Bill.
> ii. What John persuaded the doctor of was that he should examine Bill.

Notice also that the sentences behave differently with respect to the passive:

> (8) i. John expected Bill to be examined by the doctor.
> ii. John persuaded Bill to be examined by the doctor.

Here (8i) is "cognitively synonymous" with the active sentence in

---

6. The differences in the deep structures of the examples in (4) are "triggers" for the question and negation transformations. These triggers are necessary for two reasons: the correct semantic interpretation of questions and negations, and the application of the proper question and negation transformations. Needless to say, the triggers are elements which are erased in the course of the application of these "proper question and/or negation transformations," since they do not occur in the surface structure of questions and negations.

7. Ungrammatical sentences are preceded by an asterisk (*).

(5i), but (8ii) is *not* congnitively synonymous with the active example in (5ii). That is, both in (5i) and in (8i) "John expects" the same act, namely, that "the doctor will examine Bill." But in (5ii) "John" persuades "the doctor," while in (8ii) "John" persuades "Bill," that is, the action of the verb "persuade" is directed toward two different people, while the action of "expect" is directed toward the same event.

To have a theory of language it is undoubtedly necessary that transformations are stated in such a way that in the course of a derivation they can only apply to identical structures, because if transformations do not have this restriction the result will be not a theory of language but chaos. Such a restriction, however, amounts to saying that the two sentences in example (5) have different deep structures. To be exact, the deep structures can be represented in this way:

(9)   i. John expected $_{\text{OBJECT}}$ [the doctor (will) examine Bill]

     ii. John persuaded the doctor $_{\text{COMPLEMENT}}$ [the doctor (will) examine Bill]

The representation in (9ii), incidentally, shows that example (5ii) contains a syntactic structure which is not representable *in principle* by a grammar which contains only a surface structure, namely, items which have a double function. Notice that the representation in (9ii) has the phrase "the doctor" twice, once as object of "persuade," and once as subject of "examine." The surface structure, exemplified in (5ii), has only one occurrence of the phrase "the doctor"; in the sentence

(5) ii. John persuaded *the doctor* to examine Bill,

the phrase "the doctor" has, therefore, a double function: object of "persuade" and subject of "examine."

The foregoing excursion into linguistic theory was intended to demonstrate the need for a theory of language which contains, in addition to a semantic component, a syntactic component with two levels (deep structure and surface structure) plus a way of getting from one level to the other (transformations). Before turning to the question of how such a theory of language applies to the explicit testing theory proposed earlier in this monograph, it is necessary to discuss briefly the concept *rule* as used in linguistic theory. In connection with grammar, the term rule is familiar to most of us as the admonition of English teachers not to say "ain't," and similar rules. The linguist, however, uses the term rule in the same sense as the mathematician uses it. That is, transformations, for example, are called rules. In general, then, we can say that getting from one step in the derivation of a sentence (phrase, etc.) to the next is accomplished by the application of a rule. Now, however, notice that deep structures must be derived from some even more abstract structures. That is, linguistic theory cannot assume that deep structures simply exist, because there are relationships between deep structures as well as between surface structures. Because deep structures are entities of a type different from surface structures, it follows that deep structures must be derived by rules of a type different from the rules used to derive surface structures. Specifically, it has been stated that deep structures are fully explicit, in the sense that they contain *all* the information necessary for the transformational rules and for the semantic interpretation. From this it follows that the phrase-structure rules (the rules used to derive deep structures) must be stated in such a way that they cannot, in principle, lose any information, allow any ambiguities, etc.

The theory of language sketched in the preceding section has the following form:

1. Deep structure
   Derived by application of phrase-structure rules
   Contains all information necessary for semantic interpretation and transformational rules

2. Surface structure
   Derived by application of transformational rules
   Has lost much of the information present in the deep structure because transformational rules mutilate strings in the mapping process

How can this theory of language be usefully applied to the explicit testing theory formulated earlier? The answer to this question is reasonably clear. If the testing theory tries to measure the student's comprehension of instructional materials by asking him questions about the contents of these materials, then a linguistic theory that provides an explicit account of the relationships between sentences is a useful tool in the application of the testing theory. The linguistic theory not only provides the user of the testing theory with explicit definitions of the various types of questions he can ask the student concerning the instructional materials; it also provides the user of the testing theory with explicit rules (in the sense discussed above) for deriving the various types of questions.

To provide these rules it is, of course, necessary to go beyond the few simple question transformations mentioned in the discussion of the examples (4); in fact, it proved necessary to treat a large part of the syntactic component of English. It goes without saying that the remaining sections of this chapter could not possibly contain an explicit account of "a large part of the syntactic component of English." In the sense that transformational-generative grammar is such an explicit account there was neither intention nor need to provide an explicit account of this type. What has been done, rather, is to provide an account which is explicit enough so that the native speaker (in this case the user of the testing theory), using his intuitive knowledge of English syntax, can operate the fragment of English grammar found in the following sections as if it were an explicit grammar of English. The difference between this grammar and a transformational-generative grammar is that the latter does not permit the use of intuition but demands the statement of rules that are explicit enough so that a computer can use them.[8]

There are several reasons why a grammar which is explicit in the transformational-generative sense is not desirable for our present purposes. First, there is no attempt here to analyze English for hitherto unsuspected relationships, or to make explicit relationships intuitively felt to exist. Rather, the fragment found in the following sections is an application of transformational-generative grammar to a specific problem, namely, testing theory. Second, a fully explicit transformational-generative grammar of English would be a technical, complex, and extremely long work, and it would force the reader not familiar with transformational-generative grammar to acquaint himself with many concepts and conventions, and with much data, before he could understand the discussion. Third, transformational-generative grammar is an algorithm for deriving surface structures from deep structures; that is, it has as its input an abstract symbol #S#, and as its output the surface structure of sentences. The testing theory, on the other hand, may have as its input the surface structures of the instructional mate-

---

8. The reason for this constraint has nothing to do with machine translation or with machine languages, incidentally, but with the fact that valid generalizations about language can best be tested by such explicit rules.

rials to be tested. In other words, to apply transformational-generative grammar to the testing theory, we must first arrive at the deep structures underlying the surface structures of the instructional materials. Only then can we transform these deep structures into the surface structures of the questions to be asked the student. Transformational-generative grammar, however, does not provide an algorithm for deriving deep structures from surface structures; in fact, transformational-generative linguists claim that no such algorithm exists.

The fragment of English grammar presented below is divided into the following five sections:

1. Parts of Speech Analysis
2. Transformational Analysis
3. Sentence Types
4. Anaphora Analysis
5. Intersentence syntax

The first section, "Parts of Speech Analysis," deals with the co-occurrence and substitution restrictions and classifies the major parts of speech (nouns, verbs, and adjectives) according to these restrictions. This section is included to provide an explicit tool which enables the test writer to classify all major parts of speech with respect to their co-occurrence and substitution restrictions. It should prove particularly useful in constructing tests which include semantic changes, since the form classes defined by these types of restriction will ensure that the item substituted by the test writer is of the same class as the original item, that is, that it takes the same restrictions as the original item.[9] In addition, the section should also prove useful in constructing tests of the "fill-in-the-blank" variety, since it gives an immediate check on the grammaticality of the test sentences.[10]

The second section, "Transformational Analysis," is the most important part of this appendix, because it contains the instructions for deriving the deep structures from the instructional material, and for

9. For detailed instructions on the application of (the criteria of) each section, see the introduction preceding each of the sections.
10. For readers interested in applying cloze tests of comprehension, there is a further use for this section. It has been noted before that errors in cloze tests are of two kinds: syntactic and semantic. It is interesting to note that the semantic errors can easily be separated from the syntactic ones by using this section. If the word inserted by the subject falls into the same form class as the original word, the error is semantic. If, on the other hand, the inserted word belongs to a different form class, the error is syntactic.

deriving the surface structures of the test material—by reversing the process indicated in the analysis. Without knowledge of the deep structure it is not always possible to correctly identify the type of sentence structure in question. More important, however, without knowledge of the transformations involved, it is impossible to state explicitly the relationship between the instructional material and the test material.

The third section, "Sentence Types," deals, as the name implies, with the types of sentences possible in English. This section is necessary because, on the one hand, restrictions are often on structures larger than words, a fact which the "Parts of Speech Analysis" cannot capture; while, on the other hand, the "Transformational Analysis" deals with the way to derive deep structures from surface structures (and vice versa) and thus says nothing about the types of input into the transformational rules. This section thus fills the gap between sections 1 and 2. It should prove useful in constructing tests of all types, because it enables the test writer to classify the structures of the instructional material from which he makes up his test materials. He needs such a classification, because in some types of testing he must construct his test sentence(s) in such a way that they remain of the same sentence type (as per this classification) as is (are) the sentence(s) in the instructional material.

The fourth section, "Anaphora Analysis," deals with the relationship between anaphoric expressions and their antecedents. It gives a classification of the different types of anaphora, and a simple measure of their complexity. This analysis is neither as well motivated, nor as tightly constrained, as the preceding analyses, because comparatively little is as yet known about anaphora. One reason for our ignorance in this area is that anaphora is partly syntactic and partly semantic, so that grammarians feel that any solution of the problem must await a systematization of semantics, which today is far from being realized. The section should, however, prove useful to the test writer in helping him to identify and classify anaphoric expressions both in the instructional materials and in the test materials.

The fifth section, "Intersentence Syntax," deals with the syntactic relationships between sentences. Like the preceding section, this analysis gives a classification of the different types of relations between sentences, and a simple measure of their complexity. Also like the preceding section, the analysis is still somewhat tentative, since at present as little is known about intersentence relations as about anaphora. The reason for this, however, is not that intersentence relations are semantic in nature, or at least no more so than are within-sentence relations. The reason for our ignorance in this particular area is, rather, that linguists are still far from having explored the area of within-sentence syntax; and since they consider this to be the first aim of any grammar, they have simply not yet concerned themselves with larger-than-sentence relationships that obtain between sentences.

In the conclusion of this introductory section, I should like to discuss briefly the original purpose for which the fragment of English grammar described below (henceforth "the grammar") was developed. As was already indicated, grammars are not generally written for use in testing theory, or for any purpose other than to describe the structures of the language in question. This is also true of this grammar, which was developed to measure the linguistic complexity of all types of materials. Although, in its present form, the grammar applies only to written language samples of English, it is a fairly simple matter to evolve criteria which will screen out the various types of errors and mistakes that occur in spoken language, and then to apply the grammar to both spoken and written language samples. In fact, the "Transformational Analysis" (see below) has been extended in the manner indicated and applied to a fairly large sample of spoken language (for details, see the introduction to that section).

Specifically, the grammar was developed to measure the linguistic complexity, in terms of the parameters outlined in each section, of instructional materials and of the students' linguistic capabilities. As to instructional materials, it was argued that if the linguists' claim to a "psychological reality" of the theoretical constructs posited by linguistic theory are correct, this assumption should be reflected in the difficulty experienced in comprehending structures containing the various theoretical constructs. This assumption was tested originally on the materials of J. Bormuth's *Readability Project* (forthcoming), and subsequently on various other materials used at the Southwest Regional Laboratory for Educational Development and Research. All materials analyzed by the grammar were scaled by cloze tests and by intuitive difficulty ranking. There was a high correlation between difficulty measured by cloze scores and syntactic complexity measured by the grammar (Bormuth, *Readability Project,* forthcoming; Aquino and Brown 1966). In determining the student's linguistic capabilities, samples of students' writing and conversations were analyzed. Grade levels were, of course, taken into consideration. To arrive at a clearer picture of the linguistic capabilities of the children, elicitation methods were also used. This was done, for example, by showing them pictures and asking them to describe what was happening. Needless to say, direct elicitation of the form "Can you say _____?" is not possible with children; in fact, it should be avoided with all informants (subjects), although linguists sometimes use it on themselves or on each other as a convenient shortcut.

1. PARTS OF SPEECH ANALYSIS

It has long been recognized that the traditional parts of speech classification is not fine enough to account for many of the word classes a speaker/hearer commands. The analysis below is an attempt to incorporate the findings of modern linguistics into the parts of speech analysis. Class membership of words can be of two types: substitution class and co-occurrence class. The former applies to nouns and verbs only and means simply that all words that can be subtituted for by the same pro-form belong, in some sense, to the same class. Criteria for noun substitution are membership in the class [±HUMAN] and [±MASCULINE]. [+HUMAN] nouns are substituted by *who* in questions and relative clauses, while [−HUMAN] nouns are substituted by *what* and *which* respectively in these structures. [+MASCULINE] is substituted by *he,* [−MASCULINE] is substituted by *she.* Note, incidentally, that the feature [+MASCULINE] is hierarchical with respect to the feature [+ANIMATE]; that is, [−ANIMATE] is never marked by gender and always has *it* as its pronoun.

Examples of noun substitution classes:

(1) [±HUMAN]
    i. The boy lay on a stone.
    ii. The girl lay on a stone.
    iii. Who lay on a stone?
    iv. The jacket lay on a stone.
    v. What lay on a stone?

(2) [±MASCULINE]
    i. The boy lay on a stone.
    ii. He lay on a stone.
    iii. The girl lay on a stone.
    iv. She lay on a stone.

The criterion for verb substitution is stative/nonstative. The latter, but not the former, can be substituted by *do*. Note that in all sentences except those containing a *be* the whole verb phrase can be substituted by *do so,* so that the latter substitution is not a test.

(3) [±STATIVE]
    i. John ate the cabbage and Bill *did* it too.
    ii. *John knew the answer and Bill *did* it too.
    iii. John ate the cabbage and *so did* Bill.
    iv. John knew the answer and *so did* Bill.

Co-occurrence is applicable to all parts of speech with which we are concerned here. The term means that all words which can co-occur with the same type of word or with the same grammatical construction belong to the same class. In general the criteria for co-occurrence classes vary, but basically our approach here is the same as that of Harris (1957), in that a frame is assumed into which the word in question is inserted. If the resulting sentence (or phrase) is grammatical (though not necessarily semantically acceptable), the word is said to belong to the class in question; if the word does not result in a grammatical structure, the word does not belong to the class. In the body of the paper, frames and substitution items for all the classes are suggested. Needless to say, they are not the only possible frames.

Nouns can be divided into count/mass, common/proper, and abstract/concrete by co-occurrence. Below are some examples of co-occurrence frames:

(4) There was a _____.
Any noun fitting into this frame is a count noun.

(5) The _____ is here.
Any noun fitting into this frame is a common noun. Note that proper nouns like *The Hague,* if substituted into this frame would yield,

(6) *The *The Hague* is here.
Note also that in certain contexts a proper noun can be preceded by the definite article *the* if it is followed by a restrictive relative clause:

(7) The John who is in my English class . . .
In this case, however, *John* is not a proper noun, because the

speaker is defining a certain John from among the set of Johns he knows, in the same way as:

(8) The boy who is in my English class . . .
defines a certain boy from among the set of boys the speaker knows.

The co-occurrence restrictions with abstract/common nouns are more complex. The criterion here is that abstract nouns do not co-occur with certain verbs and adjectives, for example, with the so-called *verbs of the senses* such as *see, hear, watch,* etc., and with adjectives describing observable states, such as *dark, tall, deep,* etc.

(9) I saw/heard/watched/etc., (the) _____ . . .
The dark/tall/deep/etc., _____ . . .
Any nouns fitting into these frames are concrete.

PROCEDURES

Below I have outlined some procedures which we have found useful in our analyses, in the hope that the reader may find them at least suggestive. As with frames and substitution procedures, these are only suggestions. In general, we have listed words in columns and set up pairs of oppositions for each class, since class membership is binary; that is, a word either belongs or does not belong to a given class—there is no middle ground. The pairs were marked (+) and (−). Here are some sample entries:

	N	COUNT	CONCR	ANIM	HUMAN	MASC	PROP
Boy	+	+	+	+	+	+	−
Water	+	−	+	−	−	−	−
Democracy	+	+	−	−	−	−	−
Cat	+	+	+	+	−	−	−
Teacher	+	+	+	+	+	+	−

Water, incidentally, is also a verb and must therefore also be entered into the appropriate columns there. Because the classes for the three types of lexical items have nothing in common, we have found it best to use different tables for each class.

Neither so-called function words (*of, for, to, the,* etc.) nor one-word adverbs (*yesterday, about,* etc.) have been included in this analysis, because they belong to closed, numerically small sets, and lists of them can be found in various sources (e.g., Fries, *The Structure of English*).

The analysis below will be concerned only with the so-called lexical items, that is, nouns, verbs, and adjectives.

For each word in question, the analyst therefore first decides whether it is a lexical item. If it belongs to the class of lexical items, he then decides to which class (noun, verb, or adjective) it belongs.

If the word in question belongs to more than one part of speech—*walk, sail, man, run, desert, address,* etc.—it should be entered in both places.

Derived words—*arrival, expectation, observable, painting,* etc.—should be entered both for their underlying words and for their derived words.

Words belonging to more than one class within the same part of speech should also be entered once for each category. For example, *have* in: *John had me paint the window* and *John had five dollars; make* in: *John made me paint the window* and *John made five dollars.*

THE FRAMES[11]

It has been shown by Chomsky and other researchers that automatic application of both co-occurrence and substitution frames is not possible if the investigator expects his classes to remain reasonably sharp as well as formally reasonable. This is due to two facts: on the one hand, if the instructions are applied literally, the classes will often be too small for formal criteria; on the other hand, the investigator can often stretch the context a little and as a result obtain classes that are formally too large. Examples relevant to these observations will be discussed with the frames below. Here I can only say that we have tried to compensate for the facts by making up more than one frame for each class, and that, to my knowledge, all the words of a given class fit at least one of the frames given.

Analysts should also be warned against forcing frames or stretching contexts.

Nouns

(10) *Proper/Common:* The _____ is ... (−)
                      (singular)

            A _____ is ... (−)
                 (singular)

11. I wish to express my gratitude to Evelyn Hatch, who made up the frames in this section. The responsibility for any mistakes is, of course, mine, since the frames are based on my criteria.

Examples: *The John is ... (+)   The country is ... (−)

         *The America is ...   A country is ... (−)

         (+)   The John I know is ...

         The boy is ... (−)   (−)

         A boy is ... (−)   The New York of my

                           youth is ... (−)

Exceptions which do not fit the first frame should be caught by the second:

The Hague is ...   **A* the Hague is ...

The USA is ...   **A* the USA is ... (USA, USSR, UAR, etc.)

The Nile is ...   **A* the Nile is ... (all rivers)

(11) *Mass/Count:* Many _____ are ... (−)
                 (plural)

          Much _____ is ... (+)
                (singular)

Examples: *A dust is ... (+)   A boy is ... (−)

         *Many dusts are ...   Many boys are ...

         (+)   (−)

         *A few dusts are ...   A few boys are ...

         (+)   (−)

         *Much dust is ... (+) *Much boy is ... (−)

         A little dust is ... (+) *A little (not the adjective) boy ... (−)

Most mass nouns can be put into (or forced into) a count frame, *but* there is also a change of meaning when this is done. For example:

There is *much* ice cream in the freezer.

There are *many* ice creams in the freezer (those made by Safeway, those made by Ralph's, etc.).

There is *much* grain on the market.

There are *many* grains on the market.

Most of these are from "many kinds of." Some, however, have genuine specialized meanings and probably should be considered separate word meanings.

There is *much* iron in the factory. (mass)

I have *many* irons (a steam iron, a dry iron, etc.). (count)

They manufacture *much* glass each year. (mass)

There are *many* glasses on the shelf. (count)
There is *much* wood on the market. (mass)
There are *many* woods in that part of the country. (count)

Conversely, some count nouns can also be changed to mass nouns if one works hard enough at it.

There are *a few* eggs in the box. (count)
He has *a little* egg on his tie. (mass)

For the sake of the analysis, eliminate the "many kinds of" group by marking them as mass nouns. Those which have the specialized meaning change should be listed twice. The last example (changing count to mass by forced context) should be ignored.

(12) *Divisible/Nondivisible:* The _____ scattered
    ... (+)   ([+ANIMATE] singular)

By limiting the frame to [+ANIMATE] nouns, the following examples are excluded from the group:

    The rice (was) scattered ...
    The corn flakes (were) scattered ...
    The paths scattered ...

Examples: The tribe scattered ... (+)
              The team scattered ... (+)
              The people scattered ... (+)
              The herd scattered ... (+)
              *The boy scattered ... (−)
              *The pencil scattered ... (−)
              The boy*s* scattered ... (−)

(13) *Abstract/Concrete:* A $\begin{Bmatrix} \text{piece of} \\ \text{part of} \end{Bmatrix}$ the _____ is ... (−)

He _____ the _____ with a ham-
     (verb)
mer. (−)

The frames are not really adequate for the job since concrete nouns can be made abstract, and abstract nouns concrete, by the speaker. The old frame "Here is a _____; it's a _____" may be just as helpful as those listed above. The frames listed, however, will give us better agreement with categories 23 and 24, since abstract nouns take neither partitive nor instrumental.

Examples: A piece of the box . . . (−)
*A piece of the hope . . . (+)
I made the box with my hammer . . . (−)
*I made the belief with . . . (+)

(14) *Animate/Inanimate:* The _____ ate the food. (+)

Examples: The dog ate the food. (+)
*The hand ate the food. (−)
The team ate the food. (+)
*The cars ate the food. (−)

(15) *Human/Nonhuman:* The _____ wrote a letter. (+)

For story purposes, many nouns are humanized. Stories allow dogs, cats, horses, etc., to think and perhaps even write letters.

Examples: The teacher wrote a letter. (+)
*The cat wrote a letter. (−)

(16) *Masculine/Feminine:* The _____ ate *his* lunch. (+)
The _____ ate *her lunch.* (−)

Such unmarked nouns as *teacher, captain, psychologist,* etc., can be marked as both. Those nouns that take *its* in the above frame may be marked positively for 14.

Examples: The man ate his lunch. (+)
The girl ate her lunch. (−)
The teacher ate his/her lunch. (±)

(17) COMP*lement-time:*[12] The _____ on Friday . . . (+)
(event)

The frame should screen out [−EVENT] nouns such as *democracy,* etc.

Examples: The party on Friday . . . (+)
The accident on Friday . . . (+)
*The boy on Friday . . . (−)
*The democracy on Friday . . . (−)

(18) COMP—*that:* The ____ that he came surprised me . . . (+)
(fact)

---

12. New terms are introduced in full but will be abbreviated on further occurrence by using the letters capitalized when the terms are introduced. Thus, the term above will be abbreviated COMP.

The frame should screen out time words like *Sunday,* with the [+fact].

Examples: The fact that he came . . . (+)
*The time that he came . . . (−)
The idea that he came . . . (+)
*The Sunday that he came . . . (−)

(19) COMP—INF*intival:* His _____ to arrive early . . . (+)
(decision)

Examples: His decision to arrive early . . . (+)
*His anticipation to arrive early . . . (−)
*The Sunday to arrive early . . . (−)
His pledge to arrive early . . . (+)
His wanting to arrive early . . . (+)

(20) COMP—*of ing:* His _____ of arriving early . . . (+)

Examples: His idea of arriving early . . . (+)
His hope of arriving early . . . (+)
*His decision of arriving early . . . (−)
*His wanting of arriving early . . . (−)

(21) COMP—POSS*essive:* The _____ of the man . . . (+)

The frame gives some unnatural sentences, particularly with pronouns, but a rule changes the "of the man" to "the man's. . . ." What is important is that proper nouns and *-ing* forms can be screened out. This can be done automatically by marking all nouns except [+PROPER] as +21.

Examples: The house of the man . . . (+)
The car of the man . . . (+)
*Mary of the man . . . (−)
*John of the man . . . (−)
The arrival of the man . . . (+)
*The wanting of the man to go . . . (−)

(22) COMP—BEN*efactive:* The _____ for the boy was . . . (+)

Once again the frame may give unnatural-sounding sentences. What is important is that [+PROPER] nouns be excluded, which again is automatic: [+PROPER] is −22.

Examples: The food for the boy . . . (+)
The home for the boy . . . (+)
*The John for the boy . . . (−)

(23) COMP—INSTR*umental:* He hit (the) _____ with a hammer.

The class is also automatic *if* 13 (abstract/concrete) are marked correctly. [+ABSTRACT] will be [−COMP INSTR].

Examples: He hit the window with a hammer ... (+)
*He hit the idea with a hammer ... (−)

(24) COMP—PART*ive:* The $\begin{Bmatrix} \text{piece} \\ \text{part} \end{Bmatrix}$ of the _____ ... (+)

The category is automatic if [+ABSTRACT] has been correctly marked. [+ABSTRACT] will be [−COMP PART]; all other nouns are [+COMP PART].

Examples: The piece of the house ... (+)
The part of the play ... (+)
*The piece of the friendship ... (−)

Adjectives

All adjectives are to be marked as [−PROPER]. Appellations like *Big John* are not being considered in this analysis.

(25) *Mass/Count:* The _____ water ... (+)
The _____ pencils ... (−)

If semantic reasons seem to make the frame difficult, try other mass nouns (*ice cream, rice, jewelry,* etc.) for (+); and other count nouns (*apples, nickels, chairs,* etc.) for (−).

Examples: The dirty water ... (+)
*The numerous water ... (−)
The many pencils ... (+)
The yellow water/pencils ... (±)

(26) *Abstract/Concrete:* The _____ February ... (+)
The _____ school ... (+)
The _____ thought ... (+)

Since the abstract nouns reduce to three items (time, institution, and "semantic" abstracts) in the above frames, *any* of these three equals [+ABSTRACT]. Although the abstract-noun category is not well defined in these frames, I decided to retain it because it classifies verbs taking a sentential subject or a sentential direct object. That is, any verb that takes such sentential forms also takes an abstract noun in these slots.

Examples: The coldest February . . . (+)
The best school . . . (+)
The happy thought . . . (+)
*The last February . . . (−)
*The tall school . . . (−)
*The green thought . . . (−)

(27) *Animate/Inanimate:* The _____ $\begin{Bmatrix} \text{group (of animals)} \\ \text{animal} \ldots \end{Bmatrix}$ (+)

The _____ box . . . (−)

Examples: The hungry animal . . . (+)
*The hungry box . . . (−)

(28) *Human/Nonhuman:* The _____ person . . . (+)
The _____ machine (−)

Examples: The intelligent person . . . (+)
*The leather person . . . (−)
The tall person/plant . . . (±)

(29) *Masculine/Feminine:* The _____ man . . . (+)
The _____ woman . . . (−)

Examples: The pregnant woman . . . (−)
*The pregnant man . . . (−)
The buxom woman . . . (−)
*The buxom man . . . (−)
The handsome man . . . (+)
The tall man/woman (±)

(30) *Inalienable:* $\begin{Bmatrix} \text{He} \\ \text{She} \\ \text{It} \end{Bmatrix}$ is being _____ now . . . (−)

Examples: He is being honest now . . . (−)
He is being sorry now . . . (−)
*He is being tall now . . . (+)
*He is being husky now (+)

(31) *-er (-est)/more (most):* It's more _____ . . . (−)
It's _____ -er . . . (+)

Examples: It's more beautiful . . . (−)
It's taller . . . (+)

*It's beautifuller ... (−)
*It's more tall ... (+)

(32) *Passive/Active:* The NOUN was _____ $\left\{\begin{array}{l}\text{-en}\\\text{-ed}\end{array}\right\}$ by ... ;

It's a _____ NOUN ... (+)

The adjective *must* fit *both* slots in order to be marked [+ PASSIVE].

Examples: The window was broken by ... a broken window ... (+)
*The girl was pretty by ... a pretty girl ... (−)
The window was opened by ... an opened window ... (+)
*The window was open by ... an open window ... (−)

(33) *Obligatory/Optional Passive Modification:* The _____
(passive)
NOUN ... (−)

Consider only those adjectives marked [+ PASSIVE] (i.e., + 32) to see whether they must take modifiers. This seems a rather unproductive category, but we will include it anyway at present.

Examples: The trained horse ... (−)
*The fed horse ... (+)   (The *well-fed* horse.)

(34) COMP A: He is _____ to go ... (+)
Examples: He is clever to go ... (+)
He is likely to go ... (+)
*He is tired to go ... (−)

(35) COMP B: He is too _____ to go ... (+)
Examples: He is too tired to go ... (+)
*He is too likely to go ... (−)

Verbs

(36) *Object:* John _____ something ... (+)
Examples: John read something ... (+)
John expected something ... (+)
John talked ... (−)

(37) *Optional Object:* John _____ something; John _____ ...
(+)

Examples: John read something; John read . . . (+)
         *John expected something; John expected . . . (−)

(38) *Double Object:* They _____ him president . . . (+)

Examples: They elected him president . . . (+)
         They chose him president . . . (+)
         *They asked him president . . . (−)
         *They expected him president . . . (−)

(39) *Indirect Object:* He _____ something to Mary . . . (+)

Be careful not to include *for Mary;* that means *in her place.* Note that the indirect object must be [+ANIMATE]: *He sent Chicago a letter, but *He sent the boy a letter.*

Examples: He gave Mary something. *(gave, told, sent)*
         He made Mary something.
         *He anticipated Mary something.
         *He anticipated something for Mary. (Because *for* means *in her place.*)

(40) *Outside Direct Object:* He _____ Mary something . . . (−)

Test only the verbs which obtained a plus on (39).

Examples: He gave Mary something . . . (−)
         *He said Mary something . . . (+)
         He told Mary something . . . (−)

Verbs with participles will be written in as separate lexical items.

Examples: call *up,* hand *in,* read *over,* etc.

(41) INST*rumental* ADV*erb:* He _____ something with an instrument:
              (hit)
         The instrument _____ something.
                 (hit)

(The verb must fit in both slots.)

Examples: He hit something with a hammer.
         The hammer hit the thing . . . (+)
         *He bought something with a hammer.
         The hammer bought something . . . (−)
         *A place gathered with spies.
         Spies gathered in the place . . . (−)

(42) BENE*factive* ADV: He _____ it for her benefit ... (+);
not He _____ it in her place.

This should separate verbs which do not take the progressive:

cost	like	own	see	have
remember	love	prefer	understand	
know	need	forget	want	

Examples: He bought it for her ... (+)
*He advised it for her ... (−)
He took it for her ... (±)
He saw it for her ... (−)

(43) AC*companiment* ADV: John _____ (something) with Mary.
John and Mary _____ (something).

(Must fit both frames.)

Examples: John walked with Mary. John and Mary walked
... (+)
John bought something with Mary.
John and Mary bought something ... (+)

(44) *Means* ADV: He _____ it *by* (using his head).

Examples: He solved it by using his head ... (+)
*He thought it by using his head ... (−)
(He thought *about* it by ... (+))

(45) *Manner* ADV: He _____ (something) with ease/easily ...
(+)

Any adverb of manner can be used in the frame (*quickly, suddenly, efficiently,* etc.).

Examples: He did it easily ... (+)
*He expected it easily ... (−)

(46) DIRECT*ional* ADV: He _____ (it) toward $\left\{\begin{array}{l}\text{something}\\\text{someone}\\\text{someplace}\end{array}\right\}$

Examples: He threw it toward someone ... (+)
*He thought it toward someone ... (−)
He walked toward someplace ... (+)
*He asked toward someone ... (−)

111

(47) SENT*ential Subject:* That he did that _____ (to) me.

For him to do that _____ (to) me.

His doing that _____ (to) me.

If it fits any one of the three frames mark the verb +47, and if the verb fits the first of those frames, turn to (50) and mark it +50. If the verb fits the second frame, turn to (51) and mark it +51. If the verb fits frame three, turn to (52) and mark it +52.

Examples: That he did that surprised me ... (+)

For him to do that surprised me ... (+)

His doing that surprised me ... (+)

*That he did that asked me ... (−)

*For him to do that reminded me ... (−)

*His doing that walked me ... (−)

(48) SENT *Object:* Someone _____ (it) that Bill will/would sing.

Somebody _____ Bill's singing.

Someone _____ (for anybody) to sing.

If it fits any of the frames, mark the verb +47. If the verb fits the first frame, mark the verb +50. If the verb fits the second frame, mark the verb +52. If the verb fits the third frame, mark the verb +51.

Sentential objects should not be confused with purpose clauses. The latter may follow some verbs which do not take sentential objects. They can, however, be recognized and eliminated easily, because they allow an *in order to* paraphrase, which sentential objects do not. Thus, *He fought (in order) to win* and *He ran (in order) to escape the police* contain purpose clauses, not sentential objects.

Examples: Someone said that Bill would sing ... (+)

Someone promised to sing ... (+)

*Someone surprised that Bill would sing ... (−)

*Someone was my singing ... (−)

*Someone walked to sing ... (−)

(49) PREP*ositional Sentence:* Someone_____ on/at/for/etc., my singing.

or

John _____ that I sing and Mary _____ on/at/for/etc., it too.

If the verb fits the first frame, mark the verb +52. If the verb fits the second frame, mark the verb +50.

Examples: Someone protested *against* my singing ... (+)
Someone arranged *for* my singing ... (+)
John insisted that I sing, and Mary insisted *on* it too ... (+)
John said that I sang and Mary said it too. *(no prep.)* ... (−)
John ordered that I sing and Mary ordered it too. *(no prep.)* ... (−)

(50) *That* NOM*inalization:* That he went _____ somebody/something.
Someone _____ that he went.
John _____ that he went and Mary _____ on/at/for/etc., too.

A word which fits any one of these three frames is marked + 50. These should have been marked automatically by the above instructions.

Examples: Same as those for (49).

(51) INF*intival* NOM: For him to sing _____ me.
Someone _____ (for him) to sing.
John _____ (for) him to sing and Mary _____ on/at/for/etc., too.

Words fitting these frames should have been marked by the above instructions. If the verb fits any of the three frames, the verb is + 51.

(52) (POSS) *ing* NOM: His doing that _____ me.
Somebody _____ Bill's singing.
Someone _____ at/on/for/etc., my singing.

These should have been marked automatically by the instructions above. If the verb fits any of the three frames, the verb is + 52.

(53) *Identity. (Opt + /Oblig −):* John _____ (for) Mary to go;
John _____ to go ... (+)

The verb must fit both slots.

Examples: John wants Mary to go. John wants to go ... (+)
*John condescended (for) Mary to go.
John condescended to go ... (−)

(54) *Extraposed Object:* Someone _____ it that Bill will/would sing.

Someone _____ it of Bill that he will sing.

*Someone _____ that he will sing (of Bill).

The verb must fit the first frame and not fit the second frame. Verbs in this class consist of synonyms and antonyms of *like,* and the *expect* class (with *of* phrase).

Examples: She likes/hates/etc., it that he does this . . . (+)

*She likes/hates/etc., that he does this . . . (+)

I expect it of John that he will do well on the exam . . . (+)

*I expect that he will do well on the exam of John . . . (+)

(55) FOR *Deletion:* I _____ for her to do that . . . (−)

I _____ her to do that . . . (+)

Examples: I want (for) her to do that . . . (+)

I intend for her to do that . . . (−)

*I intend her to do that . . . (−)

(56) THAT *Deletion:* I _____ that he went.

I _____ he went . . . (+)

The verb must fit both frames.

Examples: I think that he went; I think he went . . . (+)

I require that he go; *I require he go . . . (−)

(57) *Passive:* $\begin{Bmatrix} \text{John} \\ \text{Something} \end{Bmatrix}$ _____ the object;

The object was _____ -ed by $\begin{Bmatrix} \text{John} \\ \text{something} \end{Bmatrix}$.

The verb must fit both frames. Verbs marked + 57 should also be + 44, so this can be done automatically if (44) has been marked correctly.

Examples: John hit the object; the object was hit by John . . . (+)

*John walked somewhere; somewhere was walked by John . . . (−)

Something broke the window; the window was broken by something . . . (+)

(58) *Sense Verbs:* I _____ him $\left\{\begin{array}{l}\text{do} \\ \text{doing}\end{array}\right\}$ it . . . (+)
   (saw)

Be careful not to include causative verbs (*allow, let, had, persuaded,* etc.).

Examples: I heard him doing/do something . . . (+)
   *I let him do/doing something . . . (−)
   (*Let* means to *cause.*)
   I watched him do/doing it . . . (+)

(59) *Causative Verbs:* I _____ them $\left\{\begin{array}{l}\text{(to) do} \\ \text{doing}\end{array}\right\}$ something.
   (cause)

Examples: I had him do something . . . (+)
   I asked them to do something . . . (+)
   I heard them do something . . . (−) (sense verb)
   I set him doing it . . . (+)

(60) *Concrete Nominal:* Verb + Suffix → Noun

Suffixes: (See Fries's list in *The Structure of English.*) Do not include *-ing* or *-ed.*

Examples: arrive → arrival
   expect → expectation
   allow → allowance, etc.

2. TRANSFORMATIONAL ANALYSIS

This transformational analysis was developed to enumerate the operations necessary to arrive at a given surface structure from the deep structure or structures underlying the former. It is important to realize that transformational-generative grammar attempts to provide an algorithm which enumerates surface structures. This transformational analysis, however, reverses the process of transformational-generative grammar, in that it starts out from a given surface structure (the sentence of the sample to be analyzed) and attempts to derive the deep structure underlying that sentence. For this reason, this transformational analysis is no algorithm, but relies on the linguistic intuition of the analyst. As stated here, this transformational analysis allows the analyst to derive both the deep structure underlying the sample to be analyzed and the surface structure of the question to be asked the student taking the test. That is, given any sentence in a sample of English, the analyst can describe how this sentence came to have the surface structure it has, and what deep structures[13] must underlie the sentence. This is done in the following way: Each sentence in the sample is run through the relevant "transforms"[14] in that list. From the examples accompanying each type, the analyst can arrive at the deep structures of the sentences in the sample. From the "operations" (these *are* the linguists' "transformations"), he can see exactly how the sentence of the sample was derived in the first place; or rather, how transformational-generative grammar describes the derivation of that sentence. Depending on the changes he wants to perform (the type of question he wants to ask the student), the test writer then applies the operations listed under the transform in question. He can, of course, again make use of the examples listed there. To minimize errors, it is advisable, at least at first, to write down the equivalents of the deep structures given in the (a)-part of the examples to each transform, since thinking in terms of deep structures needs considerable practice.

To enumerate the operations necessary to arrive at a specific surface structure, the following strategy was employed: For easier application by the analyst and for easier interpretation of the results, the transformations were grouped together in such a way as to yield different

13. Recent work in syntactic theory suggests that the structures that were called "deep structures" in, e.g., Chomsky (1965), on which this analysis is largely based, are not really deep structures but are already derived structures. I have continued to treat them as deep structures for a number of reasons.
a. The analysis has been applied in this form to a number of materials and either has been or is in the process of being validated with respect to these materials.
b. The deep structures posited in the latest research are of an even more abstract nature than are those assumed here, because they represent an attempt to account for the problem of integrating the semantic interpretation with the syntactic structure of sentences. Our present goal, however, does not lie in that direction.
c. Since the deep structures posited by the research alluded to above is of doubtful value to our present goals, I saw little point in burdening this already complex and technical appendix with the explanations of the concepts and the machinery necessary to explain and justify these deep structures and to integrate them into the work presented here.
14. Note that what I have called *transforms* do not really correspond to the linguists' *transformations.*

types of surface structures (different sentence types).[15] Each type is followed by a list of the transformations which will yield the surface structure in question from its deep structure. Thus, for example, under *questions* we find:

(1) Yes/No: 1. Invert AUXiliary   (2. *Do* support)
       3. Delete identical alternative sentence

Parentheses are shorthand for transformations not always applied. Thus, *Was John surprised?* does not make use of *do* support. This convention enabled me to generalize the sentence types.

Each sentence (surface structure) type is followed by at least one set of examples. These have an (*a*) and a (*b*) section, where the former is the representation in writing of the sentence if it has *not* undergone the transformations yielding the sentence type in question, while the latter is the written representation of the sentence after it has undergone the transformations yielding the sentence type in question. Thus, the Yes/No question above has the following example:

a. John saw the man or NEG John saw the man.
b. Did John see the man?

Where the nontransformed structure would not yield a sentence, as in the second part of the example above or in a sentence using a nominalized sentence as a constituent, a "dummy" symbol[16] (e.g., WH, NEG, NP) is used:

a. NP surprised us.   *b.* That John came surprised us.
John came.

This transformational analysis was first developed during summer 1965 for the Readability Project of J. Bormuth, who was then at the University of California, Los Angeles; and it was applied to 350 passages (2,400 sentences) of written text systematically varying in diffi-

15. The reader is referred to the introduction to the third section, where reference is made to the fact that sentence types depend in part on transformations. Notice that the section on sentence types contains many types which do not utilize any transforms and thus could not have been listed in the second section.
16. These dummy symbols correspond either to triggers (e.g., NEG, Q) or to constituents of "higher" sentences (the sentences cited in the first line of the (*a*)-part of the examples) into which the "lower" sentence (the sentences cited in the second line of the (*a*)-part of the examples) is inserted.

culty from grade-one readers to junior college texts. The materials included literary selections as well as technical and scientific writings. The analysis was then revised for the Southwest Regional Laboratory for Educational Research and Development and was applied to transcribed tape recordings of unstructured conversations collected by Carterette and Jones. There were eight groups consisting of two groups each from grades one, three, five, and junior college, with three subjects in each group. Each recording was about ten minutes in length. This material was sampled for the transcriptions made of grades one and five, and the other transcriptions were analyzed completely. The transformational analysis was also applied to E. B. Coleman's "Thirty-six Passages of Instructional Materials," which systematically varies in difficulty from grade-one level through professional level. The present version of the transformational analysis is for written materials and was revised in September 1967 in the light of the latest insights into the grammar of English by transformational-generative grammarians.

Questions

(1) *Yes/No:*   1. Invert AUXiliary[17]   (2. *Do* support)
    3. Delete identical alternative sentence

a. $\begin{cases} \text{John saw the man, or,} \\ \text{NEGative John saw the man.} \\ \text{John was running, or,} \\ \text{NEG John was running.} \end{cases}$
b. $\begin{cases} \text{Did John see the man?} \\ \\ \text{Was John running?} \end{cases}$

(2) WH: 1. WH placement   2. WH assignment
    (3. Invert AUX)   (4. *Do* support)

a. $\begin{cases} \text{Noun [+HUMAN] ate the} \\ \text{cake.} \\ \text{John saw N [−HUMAN].} \end{cases}$
b. $\begin{cases} \text{Who ate the cake?} \\ \\ \text{What did John see?} \end{cases}$

(3) *Tag:*   1. Invert question   2. Copy SUBJect and AUX
    (3. Invert AUX)   (4. *Do* support)
    a. John saw the man.   *b.* John saw the man, didn't he?

17. In these "rules," the AUX is, as usual, shorthand for $\begin{cases} \text{TENSE} \\ \text{MODAL} \\ \text{have} \\ \text{be} \end{cases}$.

Imperatives

(4) *Second Person:* (1. Copy SUBJ and *will*) 2. Delete *you*
3. Delete *will*

a. { You will leave! / You will leave! } b. { Leave! / Leave, will you! }

(5) *Nonsecond:*[18] 1. Insert *let* 2. PRO-form + OBJect

a. { We go. / We go. } b. { Let us go. / Let us go, shall we. }

Negation

(6) *Sentence Negation:* 1. NEG placement (2. *Do* support)
a. NEG John saw the man. b. John didn't see the man.

(7) *Constituent Negation:* 1. NEG placement
(2. NEG integration)
a. NEG Many people came. b. Not many/few people
came.

There

(8) *Existential:* 1. Insert *there* 2. Invert *be*
a. A man is on the corner. b. There is a man on the
corner.

It

(9) *Cleft:* 1. Insert *it* 2. *Be* support 3. Copy TENSE
4. PREDicate shift (5. Delete *that*)
a. I saw John in the room. b. It was John (that) I saw
in the room.

(10) *Pseudocleft:* 1. Insert *what* 2. *Be* support
3. Copy TENSE
a. John saw the box. b. What John saw was the
box.

(11) *Passive:* 1. Insert SUBJ into AGENT
2. Insert OBJ (or INDirect OBJ) into SUBJ

18. You will note that I put the imperative tag as a subtype of the respective imperatives. The imperative-question type is syntactically derived in the same way as other questions, except that a different intonation must be used. Since we do not account for intonation in this analysis, it was decided to subcategorize in this way.

3. Insert *be* + *en*   (4. Delete *by* + AGT)

a.
$\begin{cases} \text{Linda ate the meat.} \\ by + \text{AGT} \\ \text{John gave Bill the money.} \\ by + \text{AGT} \\ \text{Someone ate the meat.} \\ by + \text{AGT} \end{cases}$
b.
$\begin{cases} \text{The meat was eaten by} \\ \text{Linda.} \\ \text{Bill was given the money} \\ \text{by John.} \\ \text{The meat was eaten.} \end{cases}$

(12) *Adverb/Indirect Object Placement:*   1. Invert ADVerb[19]
or: (1. Delete *to/for/with/of*)[20]

a.
$\begin{cases} \text{*John gave to Bill the} \\ \text{money.} \\ \text{*John sent to Chicago the} \\ \text{letter.} \end{cases}$
b.
$\begin{cases} \text{John gave the money to} \\ \text{Bill.} \\ \text{John gave Bill the money.} \\ \text{John sent the letter to} \\ \text{Chicago.} \\ \text{*John sent Chicago the} \\ \text{letter.} \end{cases}$

(13) *Primary Conjunction:*   1. Substitute CONJunction (and, but, or)[21]   2. Delete identical and/or dummy forms[22] (herein-

19. According to this analysis the constituent "adverb" immediately follows the verb because verbs are subclassified (among others) by co-occurrence restrictions that hold between verbs and adverbs. Indirect objects and some other prepositional phrases are subclassified as adverbs for the same reason.
20. The choice obtains only with indirect objects.
21. There are two types of *and* conjunctions: symmetrical and asymmetrical (or *and then*) conjunctions. An example of the latter is, *John came home and ate his dinner.* The asymmetrical *and* conjunction is not to be counted under this heading but under *Time—After,* below. The easiest way to differentiate between the two types of *and* conjunctions under discussion here is to use the inversion paraphrase. The symmetrical *and* conjunction does not change its meaning after being inverted, while the asymmetrical *and* conjunction does. Thus, *John and Mary went home* and *Mary and John went home* are synonymous, while *John came home and ate dinner* and *John ate dinner and came home* are not. *But* and *or* conjunctions work the same way as *and* conjunction, as far as the transformations are concerned. The deep structures of these different conjunctions are different.
22. These examples are not to be confused with phrasal conjunction, which is not listed here because it involves no transforms. Phrasal conjunction can also be recognized by a paraphrase. In sentence conjunction each of the simplex sentences is true. Thus, if *John and Mary went home,* then *John went home* and *Mary went home.* But in phrasal conjunctions the apparent simplexes are not true, because the whole sentence is a simplex. Thus, if *John and Mary are a happy couple* then it is not true (nor grammatical, in this case) that **John is a happy couple* and **Mary is a happy couple.* Phrasal conjunction can also be recognized because it can be paraphrased by adding *together* to the end of the sentence without changing its meaning; thus, *John and Mary are a happy couple (together).*

after i.d.f.)　　(3. Pluralize)　　(4. *And* → comma)

a.
{
John went to the store.
Mary went to the store.
John went home.
Mary went home.
Bill went home.
}

b.
{
John and Mary went to the store.
John, Mary, and Bill went home.
}

(14) *Secondary Conjunction (and Gapping):*　　1. Substitute CONJ
2. Delete all or part of common string　　(3. Pluralize)
(4. *Do* support)　　(5. Insert *too/so/also*)
(6. *And* → comma)

a.
{
John went home.
Mary went home.

John went home.
Mary went to the store.
John went to the store.
Mary didn't go to the store.

John gave Bob a nickel.
John gave Fred a dime.

John should have been trying to leave.
Mary should have been trying to come.
}

b.
{
John went home and so did Mary.
John went home and Mary did too.

John went home and Mary (went) to the store.
John went to the store but Mary didn't (go (there)).

John gave Bob a nickel and Fred a dime.

John should have been trying to leave and Mary (((((should) have) been) trying) to come.
}

Subordinate Structures

(15) *Nouns* (possessive):[23]　　1. Delete i.d.f.　　2. Invert
3. Add *'s*
a. That hat is red.　　　　b. John's hat is red.
John has a hat.

(16) *Adjective* (see subdivisions below):　　1. Delete i.d.f.
2. Invert　　(3. POSSESSIVE change)
a. John has a hat.　　　　b. John has a red hat.
The hat is red.　　　　　　　　　　*or*
　　　　　　　　　　　　　　John's hat is red.

---

23. There is now some doubt that possessives (and others, see below) are transformationally derived (cf. Chomsky 1968).

(17) *Verbal Adjective:*   1–2.   (Cf. (16) above)
    a. He saw a child.   *b.* He saw a sleeping child.
    The child was sleeping.

(18) *Nominal Adjective:*   1–2.   (Cf. (16) above)
    Examples: Mister Brown, President Johnson

(19) *Relative Clause:*[24]   1.   Delete i.d.f.   2.   WH placement
    3. WH assignment   (4. Delete WH + *be*)
    (5. Delete *that,* WH → *what*)

a.
- The man wore a hat.
- The man came to dinner.
- The man stood on the corner.
- The man was eating candy.
- Mr. Johnson is from Texas.
- Mr. Johnson is our president.
- That NP is the tissue.
- That NP is on the table.

b.
- The man who came to dinner wore a hat.
- The man (who was) eating candy stood on the corner.
- Mr. Johnson, (who is) our president, is from Texas.
- That which (→ *what*) is on the table is the tissue.

(20) *Prepositional Phrase Adjectival:*[25]   1.   Delete i.d.f.
    2. Insert PREP[26]
    a. The man came to dinner.   *b.* The man with the hat came
    The man wore a hat.   to dinner.

Adverbs

(21) *One-word Adverbs:*   1.   Delete i.d.f.
    2. Delete *be*/verb$_\Delta$
    a. John entered.   *b.* John entered slowly.
    NP[the manner] was slow.

---

24. Recent proposals derive nonrestrictive relative clauses from conjunctions:
    a. Mr. Johnson is from Texas and   *b.* Mr. Johnson, (who is) our president,
    Mr. Johnson is our president.   is from Texas.
25. The adjectival prepositional phrase may possibly be derived nontransformationally (cf. possessives, above). The same holds true for (21) and (22) below.
26. Some prepositional phrases will fall into the categories (22) and (29). Cf. below.

(22) *Prepositional Phrase Adverbial:*   1. Delete i.d.f.
    2. Delete *be*/verb$_\Delta$ (3. Insert PREP)
    a. John entered.   *b.* John entered at one
    NP[the event] was at one   o'clock.
    o'clock.

Subordinate Sentences

(23) *Time—Same:*   1. CONJ substitution
    (2. Insert *be* + *ing*)   (3. Delete i.d.f. and CONJ)
    a. He ate.   *b.* He was eating when I
    I entered.   entered.

(24) *Time—Before:*   1. CONJ substitution

$$(2. \begin{cases} a. & \text{Insert } have + en \\ b. & \text{PRESent} \rightarrow \text{past} \end{cases})$$

    a. I entered.   *b.* He had eaten before I
    He ate.   entered.

(25) *Time—After:*   1. CONJ substitution

$$(2. \begin{cases} a. & \text{Insert } have + en \\ b. & \text{PRES} \rightarrow \text{past} \end{cases})$$

    a. $\begin{cases} \text{I entered.} \\ \text{He ate.} \\ \text{He came home.} \\ \text{He ate dinner.} \end{cases}$ *b.* $\begin{cases} \text{He ate after I entered.} \\ \\ \text{He came home and (then)} \\ \text{ate dinner.} \end{cases}$

(26) *Conditional if Clause:*   1. Insert *if*   (2. Substitute *the*)
    (3. Replace *if* and *then* by *the* and ADJective)

    a. $\begin{cases} \text{We hurry.} \\ \text{We will miss the train.} \\ \text{The tube is thinner.} \\ \text{The water rises higher.} \end{cases}$ *b.* $\begin{cases} \text{If we don't hurry, we will} \\ \text{miss the train.} \\ \text{The thinner the tube, the} \\ \text{higher the water rises.} \end{cases}$

(27) *Tense-shift if Clause:*   1. Insert *if*
    2. TENSE backshift: PRES → PAST   (3. Invert NEG)

    a. $\begin{cases} \text{I have fifty dollars.} \\ \text{I will buy a hat.} \\ \text{I am there.} \\ \text{I will see you.} \\ \text{I caught you.} \\ \text{You didn't fall.} \end{cases}$ *b.* $\begin{cases} \text{If I had fifty dollars, I} \\ \text{would buy a hat.} \\ \text{If I were there, I would see} \\ \text{you.} \\ \text{If I hadn't caught you, you} \\ \text{would have fallen.} \end{cases}$

(28) *Causal:*   1. CONJ substitution   (2. Delete i.d.f.)
  a. The man came.   *b.* The man came because he
     The man smelled dinner.   smelled dinner.

(29) *Purpose:*   1. CONJ substitution   (2. Delete i.d.f.)
  (3. Delete *in order*)
  a. The man came.   *b.* The man came (in order)
     The man ate dinner.   to eat dinner.

(30) *Although Types:*   1. CONJ substitution
  (2. Delete CONJ)
  a. It rained yesterday.   *b.* Although it rained yester-
     The children went swim-   day the children went
     ming.   swimming.

Comparative and Superlative

(31) *Unequal:*   1. COMParative substitution and placement)
  2. Delete i.d.f.   (3. *Do* support)   (4. Delete *than* . . .)[27]

  a. ⎧ John has -COMP- money.   *b.* ⎧ John has more money than
      ⎪ Bill has money.   ⎪ Bill.
      ⎨ Mary has some butter.   ⎨ Mary wants more butter
      ⎪ Mary wants -COMP-   ⎩ (than she has).
      ⎩ butter.

(32) *Equal:*   1. *As* . . . *as* substitution and placement
  2. Delete i.d.f.   (3. *Do* support)
  (4. Delete second *as* . . .)[28]

  a. ⎧ John runs fast.   *b.* ⎧ John runs as fast as Bill.
      ⎪ Bill runs fast.   ⎪
      ⎪ John runs fast.   ⎨ John runs as fast as Bill
      ⎨ Bill rides fast.   ⎪ rides.
      ⎪ I would do that (much)   ⎪ I would do as much (as
      ⎩ for you.   ⎩ that) for you.

(*That* is substituted for a preceding retrievable structure.)

(33) *Superlative:*   1. SUPerlative   2. Delete i.d.f.
  a. John is the runner.   *b.* John is the fastest runner.
     The runner is SUP fast.

27. These deletions are possible only if they are retrievable in some way from the surrounding discourse.
28. See note 27.

Complement Structures

(34) *Adjective Complements:*   1. Delete i.d.f.

 2. Insert *to/ing/that*   (3. Incorporate subjunctive

[hereinafter SJC])

a.
- She is agreeable.
- Bob SJC cook dinner.
- He is clever.
- He SJC go.
- He is too tall PREP NP.
- He SJC run.

b.
- She is agreeable that Bob cook dinner.
- He is clever to go.
- He is too tall for running.

(35) *Verb Complements:*[29]   1. Insert *(for) to/ing*

 (2. Incorporate SJC)   (3. Delete *for*)   (4. Delete *to*)

a.
- John helped.
- Bill went.
- John made.
- Bill painted the house.

b.
- John helped Bill (to) go.
- John made Bill paint the house.

(36) *Noun Complements:*   1. Insert *(for) to/ing/that*

 (2. Incorporate SJC)   (3. Delete i.d.f.)

 (4. Delete PREP)

a.
- NP surprised us.
- The fact that the solution was wrong.
- NP surprised us.
- His proposal of a solution.
- NP surprised us.
- The idea that she be dismissed.
- There is a man.
- You see the man.

b.
- The fact that the solution was wrong surprised us.
- His proposal of a solution surprised us.
- The idea that she be dismissed surprised us.
- There is a man for you to see.

Nominalizations

(37) *That:*   1. Insert *that*   (2. Incorporate SJC)

a.
- NP surprised us.
- He came.
- He suggested NP.
- She SJC leave at 1:00.

b.
- That he came surprised us.
- He suggested that she leave at 1:00.

29. According to present analyses, the only verbs taking complements are the verbs of causation (*cause, make, help, let, enable, have*—in the sense of *John had Bill paint the house*) and probably the verbs of the senses (*watch, see, feel, hear*—as in *I felt/heard/watched/saw him breathe/breathing*).

125

(38) *For—to*:   (1. Insert *for—to*)   (2. Delete i.d.f.)
  (3. Incorporate SJC)   (4. Delete *for*)
  (5. PRON + OBJ)

a. $\begin{cases} \text{NP was difficult.} \\ \text{We convinced him.} \\ \text{He wants NP.} \\ \text{He SJC go home.} \end{cases}$ b. $\begin{cases} \text{For us to convince him} \\ \text{was difficult.} \\ \text{He wants to go home.} \end{cases}$

(39) *Possive -ing:*   1. Insert POSS *-ing*   (2. Delete i.d.f.)
  (3. Incorporate SJC)

a. $\begin{cases} \text{NP surprised us.} \\ \text{He came.} \\ \text{NP is fun.} \\ \text{Someone SJC swim.} \end{cases}$ b. $\begin{cases} \text{His coming surprised us.} \\ \\ \text{Swimming is fun.} \end{cases}$

(40) *Of:*[30]   1. Insert POSS *-ing*   (2. Delete i.d.f.)
  3. Insert *of*   (4. Insert *by,* invert)   (5. *by* → *of*)

a. $\begin{cases} \text{NP surprised us.} \\ \text{The hunter shot the lion.} \\ \text{NP surprised us.} \\ \text{The hunter shot the lion.} \\ \text{NP surprised us.} \\ \text{Someone shot the hunter.} \\ \text{The hunter shot some } \begin{cases} \text{one} \\ \text{thing} \end{cases}. \end{cases}$ b. $\begin{cases} \text{The hunter's shooting of} \\ \text{the lion surprised us.} \\ \text{The shooting of the lion by} \\ \text{the hunter surprised us.} \\ \text{The shooting of the hunter} \\ \text{surprised us.} \end{cases}$

(41) *Indirect Question:*[31]   1. WH attachment
  2. WH attraction   (3. Delete i.d.f.)

30. Because *Of* nominalizations are lexically determined, there are analyses which propose to derive this type of nominalization lexically, in other words, the same way as *expect-expectation*. If this analysis is accepted, operations (1) through (4) must be deleted.

31. Quotations (questions or otherwise—as in *John said, "It's raining"* or *Bill asked, "Do you know where Oregon is?"*) can be considered nominalizations, but since no nominalization transformations are applied to the quotation, it was decided not to list them.

Nominalizations of the type *expect-expectation, arrive-arrival,* etc., are too irregular to be derived from sentences. There is often a meaning difference that cannot be accounted for; there are other irregularities between mass and count nouns (some nominals are count and others are mass, for no systematic reasons); there are irregularities in some of these nominals not having "underlying" verbs (e.g., *fact, idea,* etc.). It therefore seems best to derive these nominals lexically rather than transformationally.

a. John knows NP.   b. John knows where Ore-
    Oregon is WH somewhere.   gon is.

(42) *Extraposition:*   1. Extrapose sentence   (2. Insert *it*)

a. {
  That he came sur-
  prised us.
  That he came is for-
  tunate.
  *That he came appears.
  *She hates when he does
  that.
  The fact that he came
  surprised us.
  The house which John
  owns is in Maine.
}

b. {
  It surprised us that he
  came.
  It is fortunate that he came.
  It appears that he came.
  She hates it when he does
  that.
  The fact surprised us that
  he came.
  The house is in Maine
  which John owns.[32]
}

(43) *Subject Raising:*   1. Insert subject of embedded sentence
into the *it* of the matrix sentence   2. Replace AUX by *to*

a. {
  It appears that John is
  a scholar.
  It is said that John is
  a scholar.
  It is likely that John is
  a scholar.
}

b. {
  John appears to be a
  scholar.
  John is said to be a scholar.

  John is likely to be a
  scholar.[33]
}

32. Extraposition, which applies only to embedded sentences, places those sentences at the end of the matrix sentence. As the examples indicate, extraposition is obligatory with some verbs. Nominalized sentences must insert an *it* into the original position of the sentence, unless a noun phrase like *the fact* remains there. Note also that extraposition with *for—to* nominals is not as felicitous stylistically as it is with *that* nominals. Compare, for example, *For him to have come early surprised us* and *It surprised us for him to have come early* with the extraposed *that* nominal above. Furthermore, POSS *-ing* nominals may not be extraposed at all. For example, compare *His having come early surprised us* and **It surprised us his having come early*.

33. There is a class of verbs which allows the subject of an extraposed nominalized sentence to be inserted into the "anticipatory" *it*. This class includes the semantic class of *say* (and its synonyms), which allows the process only in the passive (cf. example above). Note that the embedded sentences yield infinitival nominals *(to)* if the subject has been removed, but *that* nominals if it has not.

As the last example indicates, this process seems to be allowed also with a class of adjectives. However, since some of the sentences with adjectives which seem to have undergone subject raising have a different semantic interpretation from sentences supposedly underlying the one with the raised subject, it is at this point

Compounds[34]

(44) *Subject—Predicate:*   1. Delete DETerminer
2. Delete TENSE + *be*   3. Invert
Madman, foodstuff

(45) *Subject—have—object:*   1. Delete DET
2. Delete TENSE + *have*   (3. Delete DET)
(4. Invert)   (5. Insert *'s*)
Artist's model, potter's wheel, apple core, armchair, ice water

(46) *Subject—Verb:*   1. Delete DET
$$\left(2.\ \text{Insert} \begin{cases} \text{-nom} \\ \text{-ing} \\ \text{-er} \end{cases} \text{for PRES}\right) \quad (3.\ \text{Invert})$$
Graduating class, flying machine, glowworm, hangman, population growth, gunshot, fighter plane, loverboy.

(47) *Subject—Verb—*NP: 1. Delete DET   2. Delete NP
3. Insert NOMinalization
Assembly plant, storage battery

(48) *Subject—Verb—Object:*   1. Delete DET
2. Delete Verb$_\Delta$ 3. Delete DET   (4. Invert)
Steamboat, air rifle, car thief, hourglass

(49) *Subject—Verb—*PREP*ositional Phrase:*   1. Delete DET
2. Delete Verb$_\Delta$ 3. Delete PREP   4. Delete DET
5. Invert
Water spot, moth hole, gunpowder

(50) *Noun Phrase—Verb—*PREP *Phrase:*   1. Delete NP
(2. Insert NOM)   3. Delete PREP   (4. Delete DET)
(5. Invert)
Gunfight, color photography

---

not clear that subject raising applies to adjectives. Thus, for example, *It is fortunate that John came early* and *John is fortunate to have come early* show the difference in meaning in that the second sentence ascribes the characteristic of the adjective *fortunate* to *John* while the first sentence ascribes it to the event expressed in the whole *that* nominal.
34. It is probably best to derive compounds in the dictionary, rather than transformationally (cf. *Possessives,* above).

(51) *Noun Phrase—Verb—Object:*   1. Delete NP
(2. Insert NOM)   (3. Delete DET)   (4. Invert)
Pickpocket, asking price, atom smashing, birth control

(52) *Subject—Verb—like + Object:*   1. Delete DET
2. Delete Verb   3. Delete *like*   4. Delete DET
5. Invert
Boxcar, kettledrum

(53) *Subject—is—*PREP *Phrase:*   1. Delete DET
2. Delete TENSE + *be*   .3. Delete PREP
(4. Delete *-ing*)   5. Invert
Washing machine, rolling pin, angleworm, grease pit

Pro-ing

(54) *Pronoun:*   1. Delete i.d.f.   2. Check [±HUMAN];
[±MASCULINE]   3. Substitute   (4. Pro + Obj)
(5. Invert)   (6. "Reflexivize")

a. $\begin{cases} \text{The man} \\ \text{The girl} \\ \text{The house} \end{cases}$ b. $\begin{cases} \text{he} \\ \text{she} \\ \text{it} \end{cases}$

(55) *Deleted Nouns:*[35]   1. Delete i.d.f.

Some—Any (in negatives and questions)[36]

(56) *In Negation:*   1. Substitute *any* for *some*
(2. NEG + *any* → *no(ne)* optional)

a. $\begin{cases} \text{NEG—Some of the girls} \\ \text{were blond.} \\ \text{NEG—You have some} \\ \text{bread.} \end{cases}$ b. $\begin{cases} \text{Not any/none of the girls} \\ \text{were blond.} \\ \text{You don't have any bread.} \end{cases}$

35. A noun can only be deleted if it is retrievable from previous discourse and is preceded by a quantifier or adjective.
36. There are two kinds of *some,* one stressed and [+SPECIFIC], the other unstressed and [−SPECIFIC]. Since the stressed *some* remains the same with respect to negative and questions, we will not deal with it here.

Similarly, there are two kinds of *any,* one meaning "any $\begin{cases} \text{thing} \\ \text{one} \end{cases}$ at all," the other is the question and/or negation form of unstressed *some.* Since the former, again, remains the same with respect to questions and negation, we will not deal with it here.

(57) *In Questions:*
1. Substitute *any* for *some* (optional if it is in the predicate)

a. { Q—You have some bread.
Q—Some of the apples were good. }

b. { Do you have any/some bread?
Were any of the apples good? }

(58) *Reciprocal:* 1. Invert *each* and DET 2. Pluralize
3. Delete noun

a. Each man saw the other man. b. The men saw each other.

Inversions

(59) *Subordinate Clause Inversion:* 1. Invert subordinate clause
(2. Insert comma)

a. { He was eating when I came.
He went although it rained. }

b. { When I came he was eating.
Although it rained, he went. }

(60) *Adverb and Adverbial Inversion:* 1. Invert adverbial

a. { John saw Bill yesterday.
His attending a party occasionally did not come as a surprise to anyone. }

b. { Yesterday John saw Bill.
His occasionally attending a party did not come as a surprise to anyone. }

3. SENTENCE TYPES

This section contains a list of sentence types that have been described by transformational-generative grammars. The assumption that this list is quite complete, except for short interjections of the type "ouch!" is based on the fact that the following materials have been analyzed using the sentence types of this section, as well as the "Parts of Speech Analysis" and the "Transformational Analysis" of the preceding sections: (1) Bormuth, *Readability Project,* 350 passages (i.e., 2400 sentences) of grade-one to professional materials; (2) Coleman, "Thirty-six Passages," of grade-one to professional materials; (3) Carterette and Jones, taped, unstructured conversations of homogeneous groups of grades one, three, five, and junior college, with three people and about fifteen minutes to each conversation.

The analysis presented in this section can be applied to surface structures, as long as the sentences in question do not contain embedded sentences. If embedded sentences are present, however, the analyst must first ascertain their deep structures[37] before he can classify them as to sentence type. An embedded sentence, as the name implies, is one which forms part of another sentence. At present, linguists do not agree on exactly which structures are reduced embedded sentences and which are not, but all agree that at least the following structures *are* derived from embedded deep-structure sentences:[38]

Coordinate Structures
- (1) i. John and Mary went to the store.
  - ii. John went to the store, but Mary went home.
  - iii. Either John went to the store or Mary went home.

Subordinate Structures
- (2) i. Although he didn't love her, John married Phyllis.
  - ii. When he came into the kitchen, he smelled the odor of escaping gas.
  - iii. Before she agreed to buy him a new coat, she wanted to know many things.
  - iv. After the students heard him, they thought he was the greatest professor they had ever encountered.
  - v. If you don't hurry, you'll miss the train.
  - vi. If I had any money, I'd buy you a nice present.

Relative Clauses
- (3) i. The boy who was wearing a red hat took my book.
  - ii. John, who was wearing a red hat, took my book.
  - iii. The boy wearing a red hat took my book.
  - iv. John, wearing a red hat, took my book.
  - v. The tall boy took my book.

Nominalizations
- (4) i. That John came early surprised us.
  - ii. For John to come early surprised us.
  - iii. John's coming early surprised us.

37. The second section contains instructions for deriving deep structures from surface structures.
38. For a more detailed discussion and more examples, see the section "Transformational Analysis," particularly the subsections on subordinate structures, subordinate and co-ordinate sentences, complements, and nominalizations.

(5) i. I expect that John will come early.

ii. I expect John to come early.

iii. I anticipated John's coming early.

(6) i. I persuaded John that he should come early.

ii. I persuaded John to come early.

iii. I persuaded John of Bill's having come early.

Complements

(7) i. The idea that John would be early surprised us.

ii. The idea of John's being early surprised us.

iii. The idea to come early had occurred to us.

(8) i. John was clever to have made so much money.

ii. John was too old to have made so much money.

iii. John was desirous of making much money.

iv. John was determined that his wife should have much money.

Some of the structures about which there is presently little agreement among linguists as to whether their deep structure is a sentence or not are:

Possessives

(9) i. John's hat is on the table;

ii. his book is on the shelf.

Prepositional Phrase Adverbials

(10) i. Mary went to the railroad station.

ii. John met Fred on the corner.

iii. Mary read the book on the table.[39]

Prepositional Phrase Adjectivals

(11) i. The book on the table was written by Mark Twain.

ii. Mary read the book on the table.[40]

Compounds

(12) i. madman, foodstuff

ii. artist's model, potter's wheel

iii. flying machine, glowworm

iv. assembly plant, storage battery

v. steamboat, air rifle

vi. moth hole, gunpowder

39. See the discussion on ambiguity in the section "Introductory Remarks."
40. See the discussion on ambiguity in "Introductory Remarks."

    vii. gunfight, building blocks
   viii. pickpocket, birth control
    ix. boxcar, kettledrum
     x. washing machine, rolling pin

Structures Containing Verbal Nouns and Adjectives

(13)   i. John's belief that Bill is a fool . . .
       ii. John's desire to go to school . . .
     iii. John's intention of going to school . . .

(14)   i. John was agreeable that he should do it.
      ii. John was desirous of making much money.

There is a certain amount of overlap between this section and the analyses in the neighboring sections. This is because, on the one hand, a particular sentence type depends to some extent on the co-occurrence restrictions of words in the sentence; and, on the other hand, a particular sentence type depends to some extent on the transformations performed in the course of its derivation. Such an overlap is unavoidable because an analysis in the form of sentence types looks at the system of language from a different viewpoint than do the other analyses. In a similar manner, two sectional views of the same object, if cut at different angles, will show an overlap at the point where the sections intersect.

Despite this overlap, however, the sentence-type analysis was considered necessary because the sentences that do not undergo syntactic transformations[41] fall into distinct types. This means that there is no way to characterize these sentence types in the "Transformational Analysis" section. Moreover, the information about sentence types, which it is necessary for the analyst to possess for certain purposes, is, as well as being incomplete for the reasons indicated above, only indirectly available from the "Transformational Analysis" and the "Parts of Speech Analysis" sections.

The analysis offered in this section is to be applied in the following way: After having ascertained the deep structure (by applying the transformational analysis), the test writer can establish the sentence type or types of the structure in question by going through the list below. Examples are included to facilitate the classification, since the names for the sentence types could not always be kept self-explanatory.

41. All structures undergo morphological and phonological rules, some of which are of a transformational nature, in that they have the same power—i.e., can affect the same changes—as syntactic transformations.

1.0   *Simplex Types*

Technically speaking, a simplex is a sentence that does not dominate another sentence in the deep structure. That is, a simplex is a sentence that does not contain another sentence or potential sentence. "Potential" sentences are sentential subjects or objects, relative clauses, and complement structures of various types.

1.1   *Simplexes without Triggers*

A "trigger" is an abstract symbol in the deep structure that triggers inversions of sentence parts that result in meaningful differences. Notice that the difference between

(15) John came to the store yesterday,

(16) Yesterday John came to the store,

is not triggered because it is not a meaningful (i.e., semantic) difference, although, of course, sentence (16) emphasizes the time adverb *(yesterday)* slightly more than does sentence (15). The same holds true for the inversion of other adverb(ial)s. On the other hand, the difference between (15) and

(17) It was yesterday that John came to the store

is triggered because (17) is meaningfully different from (15) in the sense that it is an assertion contradicting a previous assertion having exactly the same content except for a different time adverb. For example,

(18) John came to the store last week.

Sentence (15), on the other hand, can be made into a counterassertion of the type of sentence (17) only by placing an extra heavy (so-called contrastive) stress on *yesterday*. Contrastively stressed sentences are not simple statements, such as (15), despite the superficial similarity—particularly in writing—of the two.

1.1.1   *Subject + Verb*

This sentence type can have either an intransitive verb, such as *come* or *walk,* or a transitive verb whose object was deleted, such as *read* or *eat.*

(19) John came/walked/ate/read/etc.

1.1.2   *Subject + Verb + Complement*

The term *complement* is used here in its most general sense, as anything which comes after the verb. There are numerous subtypes.

1.1.2.1   *Subject + Copula + Predicate*

Aside from the transitive-intransitive classification of verbs, we must also differentiate between "copula" and other verbs—for the following reasons:

(*a*) Only copulas allow an adjective in the complement:

(20)   John is/looks/seems/appears/etc., tall/intelligent/hungry/etc.

(21)   *John eats/comes/pulls/etc., tall/intelligent/hungry/etc.

(*b*) While noncopulas allow one or more adverb(ial)s in the complement (cf. [1.1.2.4] below), copulas do not. In sentences like

(22)   John was/looked/appeared tall *in Sicily* but he was/looked/appeared short *in Sweden,*

the apparent locative adverbials *in Sicily* and *in Sweden* are really reduced time clauses *when he was in Sicily* and *when he was in Sweden.*

(*c*) Sentences with copulas cannot be passivized; that is, there is no

(23)   i. *In the corner was been by John,
       ii. *Tall was seemed by John,

from

(23)   iii. John was in the corner,
       iv. John seemed tall,

respectively.

Notice that *be* can also act as an auxiliary verb when, as in the following cases,

(24)   i. John *was* standing,
       ii. The meat *was* eaten by John,

the main verb is in the participle form: present participle for active sentences; past participle for passive sentences.

Incidentally, there is another verb with the same dual function, namely, *have*. For example,

(25) i. John has eaten the meat.
      ii. John has the meat.

Further parallels between *have* and *be* can be found: *Have* as main verb cannot be passivized; that is, there is no

(26) i. *The money was had by John.
      ii. John had the money.

The main verb of a sentence with *have* as the auxiliary verb is in the past participle (cf. [25i] above).

1.1.2.2 *Subject + Verb + Object* (nonsentential)

All transitive verbs can fit into this pattern, for example, *read, eat* (which allow object deletion) or *expect, anticipate, desire* (which do not allow object deletion).

(27) John read / ate / expected / anticipated / etc., *something.*

1.1.2.3 *Subject + Verb + Adverbial*

There are two types of adverbials, those that are selected by the verb, and those that are not. The latter are usually called *sentence adverbials,* and will be dealt with under that name here. Sentence adverbials are of two types: locative and time. All time adverbials are sentence adverbials, but locative adverbials can be either sentence adverbs or verb-selected adverbs. The truth of the latter claim can be demonstrated by the fact that both types of locative adverbials can occur in the same sentence, while other types of adverbials can occur only once in a sentence (except for sets of adverbials like "on a Monday in September of 1893 . . ." or "in 1893, in September, on a Monday . . .").

(28) i. People often eat dinner at a restaurant on Sundays in America.

Note also that it is possible (sometimes indeed preferable, as in [28ii]) to invert sentence adverbials to initial position without changing the meaning of the sentence and without the need for placing a contrastive stress on them.

(28) ii. In America people often eat dinner at a restaurant on Sundays.

iii. On Sundays people often eat dinner at a restaurant in America.

Such inversions are quite different from

(29) In the sink, mother washed the dishes.

A sentence like (29) is only grammatical in answer to a sentence asserting, for example, that "mother washed the dishes in the bathtub."[42] Both types of adverbials can be either a prepositional phrase or a one-word adverb.

1.1.2.3.1 *Subject + Verb + Sentence Adverbial*

As already indicated, this type consists of locative and time adverbials.

1.1.2.3.1.1 *Subject + Verb + Sentence Adverbial—Loc*

Prepositions: *in, on, at, by, upon,* etc.

(30) John often smiles *in England, at home,* etc.[43]

1.1.2.3.1.2 *Subject + Verb + Sentence Adverb—Time, Point*

Prepositions: *in, on, at,* etc.

(31) John smiled *at ten o'clock, on Friday, in May,* etc.

One-word time-point:

(32) John smiled *today, yesterday,* etc.

1.1.2.3.1.3 *Subject + Verb + Sentence Adverb—Time, Duration*

Prepositions: *for, in, by,* etc.

(33) John walked *for an hour, by the hour,* etc.

One-word time-duration: none

1.1.2.3.1.4 *Subject + Verb + Sentence Adverb—Time, Frequency*

Prepositions: *every, each,* etc.

(34) John smiles *every hour, each day,* etc.

One-word time-frequency:

(35) John smiles *often, frequently,* etc.

42. See also the discussion under the heading "Simplex Types."
43. Notice that these locatives often allow a time interpretation, "when in England," etc.

1.1.2.3.2   *Subject + Verb + Adverbial*[44]

1.1.2.3.2.1 *Subject + Verb + Locative*

Prepositions: *in, on, at, by, upon,* etc.

(36) John stood *on the corner, in the hall, at the table, by the river,* etc.

One-word locatives:

(37) John stood *here, there, somewhere,* etc.

1.1.2.3.2.2 *Subject + Verb + Directional*

Prepositions: *in, into, to, toward,* etc.

(38) John went *to the store, inside the house, toward the river,* etc.

One-word directionals:

(39) John went *home, inside, away,* etc.

1.1.2.3.2.3 *Subject + Verb + Instrumental*

Prepositions: *with, (by)*

(40) John ran *with his new shoes.*

One-word instrumentals:

(41) I notify you *herewith* that I intend to take possession . . .

(Note that *herewith* occurs only with a few transitive verbs having one object.)

1.1.2.3.2.4 *Subject + Verb + Benefactive*

Prepositions: *for, instead of,* etc.

(42) John ran *instead of Bill,* etc.

Note that in

(43) i. John ran for President

the *for* phrase is not benefactive but is apparently a reflex of a purpose clause:

(43) ii. John ran in order to become President.

One-word benefactives: none

---

44. To avoid overly complicated terms, it was decided to call the nonsentence adverbs, that is, those selected by the verb, simply *adverbial*.

1.1.2.3.2.5 *Subject + Verb + Manner*

Prepositions: *with, (by)*

(44) John walked *with difficulty,* etc.

One-word manner: any adjective + *ly* (and "flat" adverbs such as *fast*) having a "manner paraphrase."

(45) i. He ran slowly (in a slow manner).
ii. He ran fast (in a fast manner).
iii. He smiled winningly (in a winning manner).

1.1.2.3.2.6 *Subject + Verb + Agent*

Prepositions: *with, by*

(46) The meat was eaten *by John.*

One-word agents: none

1.1.2.4 *Subject + Verb + Complements* (nonsentential)

Most verbs allow more than one complement. One subset of these verbs allows indirect as well as direct objects.

1.1.2.4.1 *Subject + Verb + Indirect Object + Direct Object*

Prepositions: *to, of, with*

(47) I gave *Bill* the money/the money *to Bill.*

A large class of verbs fits into this pattern. Two facts are noteworthy here. First, except for a few verbs such as *say* and *explain,* the indirect object can occur either next to the verb without a preposition, or outside the direct object with a preposition, while *say* and *explain* take the indirect object only outside the direct object. Second, while most (if not all) verbs taking an indirect object may occur with a direct object only, they may *not* occur with an indirect object only.

(48) i. John gave Bill the money.
ii. John gave the money.
iii. John gave Bill.
iv. *John gave to Bill.

Note that (48iii) is grammatical only with *Bill* as direct object, and that (48iv) is acceptable as an ellipsis where it is known from the context what "John gave to Bill." Cf. *We gave at the office.*

1.1.2.4.2 *Subject + Verb + Object + Object*

(49) They elected Johnson president.

This is a small class of verbs consisting of synonyms of elect.

1.1.2.4.3 *Subject + Verb + Object + Adverbial*

Any of the sentence patterns noted under (1.1.2.2) can also occur with an object.

(50) John ate the bread on the corner. (Object + LOCative)

(51) John put the bread into the basket. (Object + DIRectional)

(52) John ate the bread at ten o'clock. (Object + TIME-Point)

(53) John milked the cow for an hour. (Object + TIME-Duration)

(54) John stopped the car every fifteen minutes. (Object + TIME-Frequency)

(55) John broke the window with a hammer. (Object + INSTRUmental)

(56) John ate the bread with difficulty. (Object + MANner)

(57) John bought the coat for Mary. (Object + BENefactive)

1.1.2.4.4 *Subject + Verb + Indirect Object + Direct Object + Adverbial*

Similarly, all sentence patterns noted under 1.1.2.2 can also occur with indirect object + direct object.

(58) John gave Bill the money on the corner. (IO + DO + LOC)

1.1.2.4.5 *Subject + Verb + Adverbials*

Moreover, most verbs take more than one adverbial—with or without direct and/or indirect objects. Obviously, it is not desirable to list and subclassify all of these separately, but rather to consider these combination(s) of the

140

adverbials—with or without direct and/or indirect objects —already classified above.

(59) John bought the tickets for Mary on Sunday at the station. (DO + BENefactive + TIME–P + LOC)

(60) Bill sent John the letter for Mary by mail at Christmas with difficulty. (IO + DO + BEN + INSTR + TIME–P + MAN)

(61) Bob drove the nail forcefully into the window frame with a hammer. (DO + MAN + LOC − DIR + INSTR)

Sentences with such a large number of adverbials may not be stylistically good, but they are certainly grammatical.

1.2 *Simplexes with Triggers*

The reason for the decision to use triggers and, in particular, to place these triggers into the deep structure, has to do with the semantic interpretation of sentences. As was shown in the section "Introductory Remarks," there is independent motivation for establishing a deep structure, and for having the semantic interpretation apply to the deep structure and not to the surface structure. Triggers change the meaning (semantic interpretation) of a sentence. Therefore triggers must be represented in the deep structure so that the semantic rules can interpret the difference in meaning characterized by the triggers. And the semantic interpretation, as has been illustrated, must be based on the deep structure.

1.2.1 *Questions*

1.2.1.1 *Yes/No Questions*

(62)   i. Did John see the man?
       ii. Has John eaten?
       iii. Did John break the window in the kitchen with a hammer?
       iv. Will John buy the coat for Mary on Friday?
       v. Should John stop the car every fifteen minutes?

Notice that any declarative sentence type can be questioned. It will therefore be best to consider *yes/no* questions as a combination of a declarative of whatever type, plus a *yes/no* question.

1.2.1.2   WH *Questions*

(63)   i. Who saw the man?
       ii. Whom did John see?
       iii. Who has eaten?
       iv. Who broke the window in the kitchen with a hammer?
       v. What did John break in the kitchen with a hammer?
       vi. Where did John break the window with a hammer?
       vii. Which window did John break with the hammer?
       viii. With what did John break the window in the kitchen?

Notice that every major constituent can be questioned by a WH word. WH questions, like *yes/no* questions, can be derived from all types of declaratives; and, as with *yes/no* questions, it is best to consider WH questions as combinations of declarative sentences (of whatever types) plus WH questions.

1.2.1.3   TAG *Questions*

(64)   i. John saw the man, didn't he?
       ii. John didn't see the man, did he?
       iii. John broke the window in the kitchen with a hammer, didn't he?
       iv. John will buy the coat for Mary on Friday, won't he?

Like the above two types of questions, tags can be formed from any kind of declarative; they will, therefore, be grouped in the same way as the above question types.

1.2.2   *Imperatives*

1.2.2.1   *Second Person*

(65)   i. Leave!
       ii. Close the door!
       iii. Close the door in the corner for me!

1.2.2.1.2   *Imperative Tag*

(66)   i. Close the door, will you (please)!
   ii. Close the door, won't you (please)!
   iii. Close the door in the corner for me, will/won't you (please)!

1.2.2.1.3   *Imperative Question*

(67)   i. Will you (please) close the door quietly!
   ii. Would you pass me the salt (please)!
   iii. Can you tell me (please) how to get there!
   iv. Could you tell me (please) how to get there!

1.2.2.2   *Non-second Person*

(68)   i. Let's go!
   ii. Let's eat the meat on the table!

1.2.2.2.1   *Non-second-Person Tag*

(69)   i. Let's go, shall we (please)!
   ii. Let's eat the meat on the table, shall we (please)!

1.2.2.2.2   *Non-second-Person Question*

(70)   i. Shall we (please) go!
   ii. Shall we get on with it!

1.2.3   *Negation*

1.2.3.1   *Sentence Negation*

(71)   i. John didn't see the man (on the corner).
   ii. John hasn't eaten.
   iii. John didn't break the window in the kitchen with a hammer.
   iv. John won't buy the coat for Mary on Friday.
   v. John shouldn't stop the car every fifteen minutes.

Like questions, all types of declaratives can be negated. Therefore, negation will again be grouped according to declarative and negation types.

1.2.3.2   *Constituent Negation*

(72)   i. Not many/few people came to the party.
   ii. John ate nothing.
   iii. John saw no one/nobody.

Justification for having constituent, as well as sentence, negation lies in the fact that both can occur, although not in the substandard sense—that is, double negation equals emphatic negative.

(73) i. Not many/few people didn't come to the party.
ii. John didn't eat nothing (I saw him eat a piece of cake).
iii. John didn't see no one/nobody (he saw Mary).

Notice that some apparent cases of constituent negation are really sentence negation; that is, the corresponding positive contains an indefinite pronoun (*somebody, something*, etc.) which would normally change to *anybody, anything*, etc., in the subject position.

(74) i. *Anyone didn't come to the party.
ii. No one came to the party.
iii. *Anything wasn't heard by John.
iv. Nothing was heard by John.

1.2.4   *Existential* THERE

(75) i. There is a man on the corner.
ii. There is a car with a man in it.
iii. There were some children in the yard.

Notice that this type of construction always has a copula verb and that the *there* is never deictic ("pointing") but simply asserts that the entity to the right of the copula does (or did), indeed, exist.

1.2.5   *Cleft*

(76) i. The man bought Mary a ticket at the station on Saturday.
ii. It was the man that bought . . .
iii. It was for Mary that the man bought . . .
iv. It was a ticket that the man bought . . .
v. It was at the station that the man bought . . .
vi. It was on Saturday that the man bought . . .

Note that, like questions, each major constituent can be put across the copula from the *it*. The effect of this "clefting" is, of course, to emphasize the constituent in the "it was/is . . ." part of the sentence. It is important to note that

(77) i. It surprised us that John came,

from

ii. That John came surprised us,

is *not* a cleft sentence but extraposition of a sentential subject.

1.2.6 *Passive*

(78) i. The meat was eaten by John.
ii. The ball was hit by the player.
iii. The troops were recalled.
iv. The house was finished.

Note that the agent of the passive can be deleted.

2.0 *Complex Sentences*

These sentences are characterized by the presence of other sentences embedded in them. It is important to realize that sentences embedded at the level of the deep structure need not be clauses at the surface-structure level. Thus, in

(79) i. The man on the corner . . .
ii. The clock on the mantel . . .
iii. The car on the street . . .

The locative phrases can be derived from reduced relative clauses. That is, the deep structure in the sentences in (79) is exemplified by

(79′) $_{\text{SUBJ}}$[the man] [$_{\text{SUBJ}}$[the man] $_{\text{COP}}$[is] $_{\text{LOC}}$[on the corner]]$_{\text{RELative CLause}}$ · · ·

where the repeated identical subject *the man* is relativized to *who* and later, along with the *be* + TENSE, is optionally deleted. There are three reasons for positing this deep structure:

(*a*) The phrases in (79) are synonymous with the respective phrases in (80) below, which are unreduced relative clauses.

(80) i. The man who is/was on the corner . . .

ii. The clock which is/was on the mantel . . .

iii. The car which is/was on the street . . .

(b) The *who/which* + *is/was* can also be deleted before a verb in the progressive sense. That is, the phrases in (81) below are synonymous.

(81) i. The man who is/was standing on the corner . . .

ii. The man standing on the corner . . .

(c) The posited deep structure and the optional reducibility of the relative clauses allows us to account automatically (i.e., without need for further machinery in the form of additional rules) for prenominal adjectives, and for the relations that hold between prenominal and predicate adjectives in almost all cases. Thus, the phrases and sentences in (82) below are synonymous and, by the proposed derivation, related.

(82) i. The tall boy . . .

ii. The boy who is tall . . .

iii. The boy is tall.

The derivation of (82i) would be the same as that for the sentences in (79), except that we need to add an "adjective pre-positioning rule."

Since complex sentences consist of one or more simplex sentences, there is no point in subclassifying the former separately, because such a classification would only repeat that done above. I propose, therefore, to consider any multiplex sentence a combination of simplex types. Note that this classification has advantages in addition to that of reducing the number of sentence types:

(a) It accounts in a natural manner for the ambiguity found in sentences like

(83) i. Mary read the book on the table,

ii. John saw the boy walking to the store,

by ascribing the ambiguity to the immediate constituency of the modifying phrases "on the table" and "to the store," respectively. If, on the other hand, we were to subclassify multiplexes, we would be forced to ascribe the ambiguity represented in (83) above to different sentence types, which is quite obviously undesirable because it is not in accordance with other things we know about ambiguity. Although complex sentences are made up of simplexes, not all possible combinations of simplexes are grammatical; that is, not all possible combinations in the deep structure will yield grammatical sentences. In particular there are restrictions on the deep structures underlying relative clauses, prenominal adjectives, the various types of complements (verb, noun, and adjective), comparatives and superlatives, etc. These restrictions are partly in the form of identity conditions, partly in the form of co-occurrence restrictions, and partly in the form of restrictions on the structure of the embedded sentence. Since the analyst will deal with grammatical (well-formed) surface structures when analyzing a language sample, I see no point to listing all these restrictions; I only wish to call the reader's attention to the fact that these restrictions exist.

4. ANAPHORA ANALYSIS

I have tried to keep the mechanics of the anaphora analysis as simple as possible, and as close to the other types of grammatical analyses as possible. In each passage, both antecedent and anaphoric expressions are marked. The antecedent is italicized and the anaphoric expression is placed in parentheses. If, as is often the case, there is a series of anaphoric expressions all referring back to the same antecedent, the antecedent of a given anaphoric expression goes back only to the last anaphoric expression; that is, an anaphoric expression can become the antecedent for the next anaphoric expression.

(1) *Pronouns* (See "Transformational Analysis" (54))

    a. Here comes *John*. (He)$_{\text{JOHN}}$ is my friend.

    b. The ocean *floor* is dark. Few fish live (there)$_{\text{FLOOR}}$.

    c. The *people* (themselves)$_{\text{PEOPLE}}$ elect officials.

(2) *Deleted Nouns* (See "Transformational Analysis" (55))

    a. The meeting was for *students*. (Few)$_{\text{STUDENTS}}$ attended.

(3) *Verb Phrase pro-ing*

    a. Mary *jumped*. Pam refused to (do so)$_{\text{JUMP}}$.

When a series of pronouns occurs, and all the pronouns refer to the same subject, the antecedent of each pronoun is taken as being the preceding one.

    a. Mary (Herself)$_{\text{MARY}}$ let me in. *(She)*$_{\text{HERSELF}}$ led me to the living room. It had been a long time since I had seen (her)$_{\text{SHE}}$.

In this classification, inverted anaphora are possible; that is, anaphora which are introduced *before* the subjects to which they refer.

    a. As (he)$_{\text{JOHN}}$ entered, *John* looked about for a familiar face.

If an entire passage is presented in the first person or in terms of the editorial *we,* inverted anaphora sometimes occur. The first occurrence of the subject pronoun is not considered anaphoric but is regarded as the antecedent of subsequent occurrences.

    a. Look at (me)$_{\text{I}}$! *I* have a new puppy. The puppy likes (me)$_{\text{I}}$.
    b. (Our)$_{\text{WE}}$ country has a birthday. *We* celebrate it on the fourth of July. (Our)$_{\text{WE}}$ country's birthday is a festive occasion.

Repetition of the same word within a passage is regarded as anaphoric. Referential repetition occurs when a word is repeated which is the same *in meaning* as the word it repeats. Formal repetition occurs when a word is repeated but carries a different meaning.

(4) *Referential Repetitional Anaphora*

    a. John ate the cake. (John)$_{\text{REFERENTIAL}}$ liked it.

(5) *Formal Repetitional Anaphora*

    a. A deer approached the pool. The *animal* took a drink. Other (animals)$_{\text{ANIMAL}}$ followed. (*Animals* does not refer directly to deer but to animals in general.)

A repeated word following a series of pronouns has as its antecedent the last pronoun.

    a. John came to dinner. *(He)*$_{\text{JOHN}}$ complimented the cook.[45] I am glad (John)$_{\text{HE}}$ liked the food.

A word can be both a referential *and* a formal repetitional anaphora in cases where it is a formal repetition of the last occurrence of the word but a referential repetition of the word as seen earlier in a passage.

45. Examples may contain anaphora other than the one exemplified. Those will be ignored.

    a. Animals entered the clearing. A *deer* entered first. The *(animal)*$_{\text{ANIMALS, FORMAL}}$ moved with grace. Other (animals)$_{\text{ANIMAL, FORMAL}}$ followed the deer.

(6) *Class-inclusive Anaphora*

Anaphora included in this classification do just what their name implies—they include a subject in some general class. This concept is best demonstrated by the examples.

    a. Johnson got up to speak. The (President)$_{\text{JOHNSON}}$ began slowly.

    b. A *horse* grazed in the meadow. The (animal)$_{\text{HORSE}}$ seemed content.

    c. The *lion* paced about his cage. The big (cat)$_{\text{LION}}$ was hungry.

(7) *Synonymous Anaphora*

This classification is for synonyms.

    a. The *country* was at war. Many citizens answered their (nation's)$_{\text{COUNTRY}}$ call for help.

    b. Mary *pushed* the button. Then Bill (pressed)$_{\text{PUSHED}}$ it.

(8) *Arithmetic Anaphora*

Words like *the former, the latter, the first, the second,* etc., make up this classification.

    a. Mary and *Bill* entered. The (former)$_{\text{MARY}}$ is a tall, lovely girl, and the (latter)$_{\text{BILL}}$ is not!

(9) *Inclusive Anaphora*

Included in this classification as words like *this, that, the idea, the problem,* etc., which refer back to an entire phrase, clause, or several clauses.

    a. Someone was pounding on the door. (This) surprised Mary.

    b. Traffic was becoming increasingly heavy. The City Council must be prepared to deal with this (problem).

(10) *Derivational Anaphora*

When a word is derived from an antecedent, it is considered to be an anaphora. Derivational anaphora can involve a grammatical class change.

    a. I *depend* on Mary. She is (dependable).

Or they can be of the same class but carry a different meaning.

    a. Mary is *dependable*. John is (undependable).

(11) *Major Anaphora* and
(12) *Minor Anaphora*

Each anaphoric word is, in addition to fitting one or more of the other classifications, either a major or a minor anaphora. For each passage, select a nominal subject. Every anaphora for this nominal subject is considered a major anaphora (11). The rest of the anaphora in a passage are regarded as minor anaphora (12).

    a. Mary was a lovely girl. (She)$_{(11)\text{-MARY}}$ had many *friends*. (Her)$_{(11)\text{-MARY}}$ (friends)$_{(12)\text{-FRIENDS}}$ liked (her)$_{(11)\text{-MARY}}$ because (she)$_{(11)\text{-MARY}}$ was kind and always willing to *help* a *person* when (he)$_{(12)\text{-PERSON}}$ needed (it)$_{(12)\text{-HELP}}$ most. (Mary)$_{(11)\text{-MARY}}$ was a good (helper)$_{(12)\text{-HELP}}$.

5. Intersentence Syntax

This section presents an attempt to deal with syntactic relations beyond the sentence level. Two facts should be noted at the outset. First, most of the syntactic relations and processes in this section are duplicated in the within-sentence syntax. Second, in order to limit ourselves to an attainable goal, we will deal only with relations that are overtly and linguistically expressed in the signal; that is, the analysis set up below will purposely ignore all nonlinguistic ways of expressing relationships between sentences.

Thus, for example, in the short paragraph below, part of the time sequence is expressed by the ordering of the sentences. That is, sentences occur in the order of events. The reader assumes, unless the writer expressly informs him that this is not the case, that the order of the sentences agrees with the order of events. This agreement of order, however, is a logical convention between writer and reader (speaker and hearer) which has no syntactic or linguistic expression other than order. Although English happens to express a number of syntactic surface relationships by left-to-right order, linguistic relationships in general are not necessarily so expressed, nor are even surface relationships in languages other than English usually expressed by order.

> John returned home late. He opened the door and entered the kitchen of his small apartment. There he found an unexpected visitor lying on the floor.

Obviously, all four sentences in the above sample are in a time sequence, but that sequence is only once overtly expressed, and even then it is not easy to recognize it as such. Sentence 2 shows a pronoun and an agreement in order; sentence 3 is coordinated but in reality has a deleted time-sequence word along with the *and* which makes the whole expression into a time-sequence phrase; sentence 4 shows a *locative* which was made into a pronoun, and the normal agreement in order.

It is similarly difficult to express the relations of topic sentences to comment sentence(s) linguistically, because these relations presently seem to be mainly in the semantics and in the knowledge of the world shared by writer and reader. The only syntactic clue to topic sentences seems to be the fact that if they contain any anaphoric expressions, the antecedents to those expressions lie outside the paragraph being analyzed. Usually, the antecedent is at least located in the preceding paragraph. Anaphora in comment sentences, on the other hand, usually have their antecedents in the paragraph being analyzed.

These observations, however, do not allow us to distinguish between coordinated sentences as opposed to subordinated sentences (i.e., comment sentences). That is, it is quite possible that a paragraph begins with a topic sentence, followed by a coordinated sentence plus a set of subordinated comment sentences. Here, we use order, because it is always the second of the two topic sentences that is coordinated to the first. That is, in a set of two coordinated topic sentences, the first will be considered the topic sentence, and the second coordinated to it, and not vice versa. This somewhat arbitrary decision reflects the practice of traditional grammarians.

One last remark on topic sentences: Topic sentences can exhibit a large range of the syntactic relations found between sentences. At this point, however, it seems unwise to take these relationships into consideration, because they seem to express relations between whole paragraphs. It is our belief, in other words, that there is interparagraph syntax which is expressed largely through the syntactic relationships shown in the topic sentences of these paragraphs. It would be a mistake to consider interparagraph syntax when dealing with intersentence syntax. We hope, rather, to develop an interparagraph syntax in the future. What will be analyzed in the intersentence syntax is whether a sentence is a topic sentence. All syntactic relations within the topic sentence are, for the purposes of the intersentence syntax analysis, either of a lower level (within-sentence syntax) or of a higher level (inter-paragraph syntax). Needless to say, they are not to be analyzed here.

As an example, let us consider the following paragraph (Coleman 1965) in which the sentences are numbered for ease of reference.

[*a*] A nobleman and a merchant met in a tavern. [*b*] For their lunch they ordered soup. [*c*] When it was brought, the nobleman took a spoonful, but the soup was so hot that he burned his mouth and tears came to his eyes. [*d*] The merchant asked why he was weeping. [*e*] The nobleman was ashamed to admit he had burned his mouth and answered, "Sir, I once had a brother who committed a great crime, for which he was hanged. [*f*] I was thinking of his death and that made me weep." [*g*] The merchant believed this story and began to eat his soup. [*h*] He too burned his mouth, so that he had tears in his eyes. [*i*] The nobleman noticed and asked the merchant, "Sir, why do you weep?" [*j*] The merchant, who now saw the nobleman had deceived him, answered, "My lord, I am weeping because you were not hanged together with your brother."

(*a*) topic

(*b*)–(*j*) comment

(*c*) time: same

(*d*) dialog: question

(*e*) dialog: answer
    time: before

(*f*) dialog: statement
    time: same

(*g*) time: after

(*i*) dialog: question

(*j*) dialog: answer
    time: same

It can be seen from this simple example that there are many inter-sentence relations that the reader must know and keep in his mind when reading a passage. This example does not use a wide range of relationships, but it should be enough to give an idea of how the intersentence syntax analysis may be applied.

Below is a list of intersentence relations. They are numbered for ease of reference. Each named relationship is followed by an operations count. As in the transformation analysis, the operations count suggests the operations the writer/reader is thought to perform when he uses the relationship in question. Relationship and operations count are followed by at least one example.

Conjunction

(1) *And:*   1. CONJunction substitution
2. Coordinate to preceding sentence

   a. John saw many cars. *And* he saw some trucks too.[46]

(2) *But:*   1. CONJ substitution
2. Coordinate to preceding sentence

   a. John wanted to buy two chairs and a table. *But* his wife thought that two chairs would not be enough.

Here, again, the sentences in question must be invertible without a change in meaning, since there is also a *but-then time conjunction*.

(3) *Or:*   1. CONJ substitution
2. Coordinate to preceding sentence

   a. It was Ruth whom John married. Or was it Harriet?

Time

(4) *Same:*   1. CONJ substitution
2. Subordinate to preceding sentence(s)

   a. John was eating his dinner. At the same time he was trying to convince Esther that they should go out together.

(5) *After:*   1. CONJ substitution
2. Subordinate to preceding sentence(s)

   a. The bus arrived at the depot. *And* it left there again.

   b. John ate his dinner. Later he tried to convince Esther that they should go out together.

(6) *Before:*   1. CONJ substitution
2. Subordinate to preceding sentence(s)

   a. John didn't eat any dinner. He had tried to convince Esther that they should go out together, but she had refused.

46. Note that in the sentences *The bus arrived at the depot, And it left there again,* the *and* is not a *conjunction,* but a *time* relationship which happens to contain *and.* This can easily be tested in the following way: If the sentences in the first example are inverted, there is no change in meaning. If, however, the sentences in the second example, shown below, are inverted, there is a change in meaning. That is, if the sentences of a *time* relationship containing *and* (the whole CONJ is *and then,* but the *then* may be optionally deleted) are inverted, either the meaning of the sentences is changed or the whole sequence is rendered semantically anomalous.

Causal

(7) *Cause:*   CONJ substitution
   2. Subordinate to preceding sentence(s)

   a. This was *because* he had managed to convince Esther that they should go out together.

(8) *Effect:*   1. CONJ substitution
   2. Subordinate to preceding sentence(s)

   a. John had convinced Esther that they should go out together. *Therefore* he ate his dinner with great enjoyment.

Although

(9) *Although:*   1. CONJ substitution
   2. Subordinate to preceding sentence(s)

   a. John managed to convince Esther that they should go out together. *Nevertheless,* he did not enjoy his dinner.

Example

(10) *Example:*   1. "Example word" substitution
   2. Subordination to modified sentence

   a. John knew many dictators. *Some of them* were Hitler, Stalin, Mussolini, Tito, Franco, and Castro.

Lists

(11) *Lists:*   1. "List word" substitution
   2. Subordinate to modified sentence

   a. There are a number of reasons for us not to consider John's proposal. *In the first place,* we do not know that he is honest. *In the second, . . . In the third, . . .*

Parenthetical

(12) *Parenthetical:*   1. "Parenthetical word" insertion
   2. Subordination

   a. John enjoyed his dinner immensely. This fact, *incidentally,* indicated that he had managed to convince Esther that they should go out together.

(13) *Explanatory:*   1. "Explanation word" substitution
   2. Subordination

    a. John enjoyed his dinner tonight. You see, he had just managed to convince Esther that they should go out together.

Topic-Comment Relations[47]

(14) *Topic Sentence*

(15) *Comment Sentence*

    Topic- and comment-sentence relationships are, as yet, largely defined by the anaphoric relationships and by the intuitive judgment of the analyst. That is, the topic sentence is "what the paragraph is all about," while the comment sentences "enlarge upon the statement made by the topic sentence."

Dialog

(16) *Statement:*

    a. John was phoning Esther. He told her that *he wanted to* take her to a movie.

(17) *Answer:*

    a. The nobleman . . . answered, *"Sir, I once had a brother who committed a great crime for which he was hanged."*

(18) *Question:*

    a. The nobleman . . . asked the merchant, *"Sir, why do you weep?"*

47. The coordinate-subordinate relationship between sentences is, at this point, not at all clear, and it was therefore decided to leave it out of the analysis for the time being. All we know now is that topic sentences seem to be coordinated with respect to each other and that comment sentences are subordinated to topic sentences. There is no way at present to decide whether comment sentences are coordinated or subordinated to each other. In other words, since at present the coordinate-subordinate relationship seems to be much the same as the topic-comment relationship, there seemed to be little point in including the former.

References

Aquino, M., and D. L. Brown. 1966. Linguistic analysis of children's speech. *Southwest Regional Laboratory Progress Report*, November. Inglewood, Calif.

Bach, E. 1964. *An introduction to transformational grammars*. New York: Holt, Rinehart, & Winston.

Bloom, B. S., ed. 1956. *Taxonomy of educational objectives, handbook I: Cognitive domain*. New York: David McKay.

Bolinger, D. L. 1967. Entailment and the meaning of structure. Unpublished paper. Cambridge, Mass.: Harvard University.

Bormuth, J. R. March 1969. Development of readability formulas. Technical Report, USOE Project No. 5-0539, University of Chicago.

Chomsky, N. 1957. *Syntactic structures*. The Hague: Mouton & Co.

———. 1965. *Aspects of the theory of syntax*. Cambridge, Mass.: M.I.T. Press.

———. Remarks on nominalization. In Jacobs and Rosenbaum, eds., *Readings in English transformational grammar*. 1969, forthcoming.

Cronbach, L. J. 1963. Course improvement through evaluation. *Teachers College Record* 64: 672–83.

Davis, F. B. 1944. Fundamental factors of comprehension in reading. *Psychometrika* 9: 185–97.

———. 1964. *Educational measurements and their interpretation*. Belmont, Calif.: Wadsworth.

———. 1967. Identification and measurement of reading skills in high-school students. U.S. Office of Education CRP No. 3023. Philadelphia: University of Pennsylvania.

Fillmore, C. J. 1968. The case for case. In Emmon Bach and Robert T. Harms, eds., *Universals in Linguistic Theory*. New York: Holt, Rinehart & Winston.

Gagné, R. M. 1967. Instructional variables and learning outcomes. Paper read at Symposium on Problems in the Evaluation of Instructions, 13–15 December 1967, University of California, Los Angeles.

Glaser, R. 1963. Instructional technology and the measurement of learning outcomes: Some questions. *American Psychologist* 18: 519–21.

Gleitman, L. R. 1965. Coordinating conjunctions in English. *Language* 41: 260–93.

157

Harris, Z. 1957. Cooccurrence and transformation in linguistic structure. *Language* 33: 283–340.

Hively, Wells, II; Patterson, Harry L.; and Page, Sara H. 1968. Generalizability of performance by job corps trainees on a universe-defined system of achievement tests in elementary mathematical calculation. Paper presented at the annual meeting of the American Educational Research Association, February.

Holland, J. G. 1967. A quantitative measure for programmed instruction. *American Educational Research Journal* 4: 87–102.

Jacobs, R. A., and Rosenbaum, P. S. 1967. *Grammar I* and *Grammar II*. Boston: Ginn.

Karraker, R. J. 1967. Knowledge of results and incorrect recall of plausible multiple-choice alternatives. *Journal of Educational Psychology* 58: 11–14.

Katz, J. J. 1966. *The philosophy of language*. New York: Harper & Row.

Katz, J., and Postal, P. 1964. *An integrated theory of linguistic description*. Cambridge, Mass.: M.I.T. Press.

Klima, E. Negation in English. In Katz and Fodor, eds., *The structure of language*, pp. 246–323. Englewood Cliffs, N.J.: Prentice Hall.

Kuroda, S-Y. 1965. A note on English relativization. Unpublished paper. Cambridge, Mass.: Massachusetts Institute of Technology.

Lakoff, G. 1965. *On the nature of syntactic irregularity*. Computational Laboratory of Harvard University, Report No. 16 to the National Science Foundation. Cambridge, Mass.

Lakoff, G., and Peters, S. 1965. *Phrasal conjunction and symmetric predicates*. Computational Laboratory of Harvard University, Report No. 17 to the National Science Foundation. Cambridge, Mass.

Lees, R. B. 1960. *The grammar of English nominalizations*. The Hague: Mouton & Co.

McCawley, J. D. 1967. Where do noun phrases come from? Unpublished paper. Chicago: University of Chicago.

Menzel, P. 1967. Anaphora. Unpublished paper. University of California at Los Angeles.

———. 1968. Complementation and historical syntax. Expanded version of paper read at Annual Meetings of the Linguistic Society of America.

Peterson, T. H. 1966. A transformational analysis of some derived verbs and adjectives in English. Unpublished paper. University of California, Los Angeles.

Postal, P. 1967. On so-called "pronouns" in English. Georgetown Monograph Series on Languages and Linguistics, 17th annual Round Table Meeting.

Rosenbaum, P. S. 1967. *The grammar of English predicate complement constructions*. Cambridge, Mass.: M.I.T. Press.

Rosenbaum, P., and Lochack, D. 1966. The I.B.M. core grammar of English. *Specification and utilization of a transformational grammar*. Scientific Report No. 1. Yorktown Heights, N.Y.: I.B.M. Corporation, Thomas J. Watson Research Center.

Ross, J. R. 1967. Constraints on variables in syntax. Unpublished Ph.D. dissertation, Massachusetts Institute of Technology.

References

Scriven, M. 1967. Aspects of curriculum evaluation. In Ralph Tyler, ed., *Perspectives of curriculum evaluation*. Chicago: Rand McNally.

Stockwell, R.; Schachter, P.; and Partee, B. H., principal investigators. Forthcoming. *The air force English syntax project grammar*. U.C.L.A.

Thomas, O. 1965. *Transformational grammar for the teacher of English*. New York: Holt, Rinehart, & Winston.

Thorndike, R. L., and Hagen, E. 1955. *Measurement and evaluation in psychology and education*. New York: John Wiley.

Tyler, R. W. 1950. *Basic principles of curriculum and instruction*. Chicago: University of Chicago Press.

Index

Abstract objectives, 18–19
Acceptability of an item definition, 10
Anaphora: postcedents, 50; anaphoric expressions and antecedents, 50–52; definition of, 50–52; types of, 51, 147–50; in multiple correct responses, 52–53
Anaphora-based items: derivation of, 50–53; multiple correct responses to, 52–53

Base sentence, 45–46
Behavioral alternations: behavioral outline, 8, 11; branches, phrase structure, 38
Behavioral hierarchies: conceptual analysis of, 75–76; diagrams and notation, 76–77; ambiguity in two stage testing designs, 77–78; analysis of item difficulty variance, 78–80; analysis of variance components in, 80–81
Behaviorally stated objectives, 18–19

Cognitive processes: in item labels, 8–9, 11–13, 24–28, 31–32; complexity of, 9, 57; taxonomies of, 9, 30. *See also* Behavioral hierarchies
Compound items, 50
Content, item of. *See* Item of content
Content analysis theory, 28–32
Content outline, 8, 10–11
Content structure rules, 58–59
Criterion reference tests: description of, 15–17; in time-trial evaluations, 20–21; in horse race evaluations, 21–23

Derived sentence, 45–46
Discourse derived items, 50–55; anaphora items, 50–53; intersentence items, 53–55; topic sentence items, 62–63

Echo items, 39–40
Empirical relevance of an item, 14
Evaluation procedures: in practical school settings, 4; formative and summative, 17–23; time trial and horse race, 20–23

Formative evaluation, 17–20

Grammar: higher level syntax, 10, 57–62; syntax in item writing, 10, 34–38; miniature, 36

Hierarchies, synonyms, 47–49. *See also* Behavioral hierarchies

Instruction derivation rules: content structure rules, 58–59; psychological rules, 59; value rules, 59–60; redundancy rules, 60–61; application of rules, 61
Instructional content theory, 28–32
Instructional programming, 17. *See also* Formative evaluation
Instructional theory: limitations on due to traditional tests, 2, 6, 25–28; uses of operational items in, 2, 5, 25–28
Intersentence questions, 53–55
Intersentence syntax, 150

161

Item of content: in ratio measurement of achievement, 20–22; instructional content, 21–22; instrumental content, 21–22

Item definition, operational: nature of, 5, 9–10, 34–35; contrasted with traditional, 10–15; acceptability and satisfactoriness of, 10, 64–65; method of developing, 56-65

Item definition, traditional: method of defining, 8–9, 10–15; subjectivity of, 8–9; contrasted with operational definitions, 10–15

Item labels, 11–13

Item response theory: nature of, 68–82; traditional items and, 6, 25–27; logic underlying, 26–27, 35; item response as a transfer task, 28

Item sampling, 15–17, 35

Item structure, 14, 62–63

Item transformations: nature of, 34–53, 64–65; distinguished from linguistic transformations, 35–36

Item types: subject deletion, 9–10, 12, 14; echo, 39–40; tag, 40–41; yes/no, 41; rote, 45; transform, 45–47; semantic substitute, 45, 49–50; semantically cued, 46; compound, 45, 50; sentence derived, 39–50; anaphora, 50–53; discourse derived, 50–55; intersentence, 53–55; topic sentence, 62–63

Item-validity theory, 82–83

Item writers, traditional: objectives of, 2; methods of, 8-ᐢ; variability attributable to, 11, 15–16, 17

Item-writing methods: traditional versus operational, 8–15; artistry in, 9

Item-writing theory: nature of, 4, 66–67; limits of, 10, 13; distinguished from test design, 13; development of, 56–65; linguistic rationale, 87–99

Logic of test item: relevance to instruction, 13–14, 18–20, 24–28, 34; in experiments, 24–28; and measurement of transfer, 28

Multiple choice alternatives, 44, 47, 52

Nodes: testable and nontestable, 22, 43; terminal and nonterminal, 37; lexical and structural, 38

Norm reference tests, 23–24

Operationalism in item writing, 4

Paraphrase transformation, 39, 46–47

Parts of speech, 99–115

Phrase structure: trees, 37–38; terminal and nonterminal nodes, 37; branches, 38; dominant nodes, 38; structure and lexical nodes, 38; terminal structures and strings, 38

Pro words, 10, 14

Psychological rules, 59

Public policy making: tests in, 1, 2, 5–6; new questions posed for testing, 2

Ratio-measurement in achievement, 20–22, 23

Redundancy rules, 60–61

Referencing of scores: criterion, 15–17; norm, 15

Relevance of an item. See Logic of test item

Response: as transfer, 28; in multiple choice items, 44, 47, 52; rote, 45; transform, 47; semantic substitutes, 47–50; anaphoric equivalence, 52–53

Rote item. See Item types, rote

Selectional features, 42, 99–115

Semantically cued items, 46

Semantic substitute: type of item, 47, 49–50; descriptive device, 47–49; including and excluding terms, 48; lexical and phrasal, 48; symmetrically and hierarchically substitutable, 48–49

Sentence derived items. See Item types, sentence derived

Sentence types, 130–46

Sentence verification items, 39–43

Standardized achievement tests, 23–24

Structures: testable and nontestable, 22, 43; terminal, 37; phrase, 37–38; trees, 37–38

Subject deletion items. See Item types, subject deletion

Summative evaluation: horse race, 20, 22–23; time-trial, 20–22

Synonyms. See Semantic substitute

Syntax. See Structures; Grammar

Tag items, 40–41

Test-by-program interactions, 22–23, 24

Test design theory: requirements of, 10, 13; criteria for, 13; distinct from

item writing theory, 13; two stage, 76–78
Topic sentence item, 62–63
Transfer, item response as, 28
Transformational analysis of structures, 115–30
Transformations: linguistic versus item, 35–36; paraphrase, 39, 46–47
Transform items. *See* Item types, transform

Trees. *See* Phrase structure

Value rules, 59–60

Wh-items: 43–50; rote, 45; transform, 45; compound, 45, 50; semantic substitute, 45, 49–50; semantically cued, 46
Wh-pro words, 10, 14, 43–44

Yes/no items. *See* Item types, yes/no